Build Your Own IoT Platform

Develop a Fully Flexible and Scalable Internet of Things Platform in 24 Hours

Anand Tamboli

Apress®

Build Your Own IoT Platform

Anand Tamboli
Sydney, NSW, Australia

ISBN-13 (pbk): 978-1-4842-4497-5   ISBN-13 (electronic): 978-1-4842-4498-2
https://doi.org/10.1007/978-1-4842-4498-2

Managing Director, Apress Media LLC: Welmoed Spahr
Acquisitions Editor: Nikhil Karkal
Development Editor: Siddhi Chavan
Coordinating Editor: Divya Modi

Cover designed by eStudioCalamar

Cover image designed by Freepik (www.freepik.com)

Distributed to the book trade worldwide by Springer Science+Business Media New York, 233 Spring Street, 6th Floor, New York, NY 10013. Phone 1-800-SPRINGER, fax (201) 348-4505, e-mail orders-ny@springer-sbm.com, or visit www.springeronline.com. Apress Media, LLC is a California LLC and the sole member (owner) is Springer Science + Business Media Finance Inc (SSBM Finance Inc). SSBM Finance Inc is a **Delaware** corporation.

For information on translations, please e-mail rights@apress.com, or visit http://www.apress.com/rights-permissions.

Apress titles may be purchased in bulk for academic, corporate, or promotional use. eBook versions and licenses are also available for most titles. For more information, reference our Print and eBook Bulk Sales web page at http://www.apress.com/bulk-sales.

Any source code or other supplementary material referenced by the author in this book is available to readers on GitHub via the book's product page, located at www.apress.com/978-1-4842-4497-5. For more detailed information, please visit http://www.apress.com/source-code.

Table of Contents

viii

About the Author

Anand Tamboli has loved solving problems in smarter ways since his childhood. As life progressed, he started to do that at scale with his entrepreneurial mindset.

Anand is a versatile professional, a seasoned entrepreneur, and creator of many innovative products & services. With his cross-domain and multi-industry experiential knowledge, Anand sees things with a uniquely different lens.

With his profound understanding of disruption and business transformation, Anand concentrates on solving customer problems while utilizing the latest technology advancements. However, he strongly believes that technology is not a panacea; it rather takes the right combination of people, process, technology, and timing to achieve the best results.

With numerous innovative products & services deployed in last 20+ years, Anand has garnered deep expertise in business improvement, business transformation, data science, IoT, cognitive systems, machine learning, artificial intelligence, etc.

Anand helps businesses to improve their key metrics by finding and solving meaningful problems in innovative ways. He constantly evangelizes and inspires people for the emerging future and encourages non-linear thinking. Sane and sensible adoption of technology remains his area of focus. Reach him at https://www.anandtamboli.com/linkedin?9781484244975.

About the Technical Reviewer

Name: Contributing Editor

Just another geek playing with digital and analog software and hardware toys since the late 1960s.

Acknowledgments

I am grateful to my entire family: my son, daughter, and wife, who are my daily sources of inspiration and energy. My humble regards to my father, who nurtured my love of books since childhood; my mother, who supported my quests; and my sister and all my in-laws, who have encouraged and supported me for all my endeavors.

My sincere thanks to the Apress team—Nikhil, Divya, and Matthew—for their continued support and helping to bring this book to life.

Special thanks to Frank and Siddhi for their careful review and helpful feedback.

Thanks to my friends who helped in the initial review of a few chapters with their valuable feedback—Peter Vinogradoff, Prof. Pradnya Kulkarni, and Prof. Dipalee Rane. Their input helped with shaping and making this book more suitable to the target audience.

Introduction

If you search for "IoT platform" on Google, it will return about 190 million results within a second. This is the level of proliferation that IoT has achieved (especially IoT platforms) in recent years. Every solution that is related to the IoT needs a platform.

Whether you develop a custom platform or buy it off the shelf means a lot to your final product. Moreover, the term *IoT platform* has many connotations, and vendors have overused it to a point where it does not convey anything meaningful.

As businesses and working scenarios are evolving, I am seeing many smaller companies delving into IoT. However, not having your own IoT platform is one of the impediments for such an evolution. The easy/lazy answer, as many would suggest, is to use freemium or free-trial platforms.

What lies ahead is a greater challenge when things scale and costs skyrocket exponentially. When the trial expires or freemium is not enough, users find themselves locked-in, and switching over is neither simpler nor easier.

Additionally, buying off-the-shelf solution often means that you subordinate requirements or retrofit things to suit what is available. You might end up building a subpar solution, if not an outright bad one. If having full flexibility and control means something to you, this book is for you.

I chose to write this book as I saw many of my customers struggling to understand the IoT platform landscape. State of the play has not been balanced with many vendors convoluting the offering to make it look like the greatest thing ever built. For short-term gains, they have raised artificial constraints and showed superficial problems that only their offering can solve. I believe in empowering customers, and this book is a humble attempt to do it.

The book is not about building a full-blown enterprise-grade system. It is about being agile in a true sense and reducing time to the market without breaking the bank. It is about designing something that you can scale incrementally without having to do a lot of rework or disrupting your current state of the work.

If you are a small to medium-sized company, or part of the development team at a non-IT company, you will find this book quite useful. If you are an independent developer, researcher, or learner, you will see the usefulness of the content for your endeavors too. Whether you are new to the programming world or have basic to intermediate programming skills, you will find this hands-on book equally useful.

The book supports the idea of being frugal at the start, and then invests only when and where necessary. It would help you to tap into technology advancements without bank-breaking budgets, and get off the ground quickly, contrary to the longer times required to adapt to the off the shelf or freemium platforms. More importantly, you will be in full control of what you are developing throughout the process.

Throughout 12 chapters of this book, I guide you through the step-by-step process of building your own IoT platform. There are must-haves and there are nice-to-haves; I will distinguish between the two and focus on how to build the must-haves. You will not only save heaps but also enjoy a control-wielding and satisfying learning experience.

In the first chapter, I discuss the necessary and sufficient qualities that any IoT platform must have and why. I also elaborate on the key question of why you should build your own.

Building your own means understanding at the ecosystem level is important; we do that in Chapter 2, where block diagram–level details of the IoT platform are discussed.

Better planning is a key to success that reduces confusion and agony later on. So, I cover a platform wish list, and the technical and general requirements for the building of our platform in Chapters 3 and 4.

The rubber actually hits the road in Chapter 5, where we initialize the cloud instance, install the required software stack, and apply security. If you are eager to jump into the "how" of building things, this is where you might want to start (and read about the "why" later).

One of the core elements of the platform is a two-way messaging system bus, which is explained in Chapter 6 along with the installation of broker software and securing it.

Building critical components of the platform, and the message broker extension with additional functionality, are covered in Chapter 7. Additional configurations and testing the core built to that point are covered in Chapter 8.

In Chapter 9, additional microservices and data access APIs are covered, along with the foundation for the rule engine. Then we build a full rule engine and authentication mechanism in Chapter 10.

In Chapter 11, we add documentation and provide the testing facility for developers with interactive API documentation.

Finally, in Chapter 15, I address a few commonly asked questions in various forums and discuss a few advancements that are in progress, which you might want to add to the platform when you build it. As I conclude, I leave you with a few possibilities to experiment.

Remember that all the code and configuration files discussed in this book are available on GitHub at `https://github.com/knewron-technologies/in24hrs`. Feel free to star, fork, or download them as you wish, and if you have more to add or suggest, I will be happy to hear from you.

I wish you all the best on this interesting journey and sincerely hope that you will enjoy the book as much as I enjoyed writing it!

CHAPTER 1

So... You Want to Build Your Own!

It's good that you are keen on building your own IoT platform, or at least you are interested about knowing what it takes to build one. For either reason, it is important to understand what an IoT platform essentially means in the general sense. First, let's look at what *IoT* means.

In this chapter, I briefly touch upon IoT's background and building our own platform in this book. I discuss the following:

- The types of IoT platforms

- The characteristics of a good IoT platform

- Why you should build your own IoT platform

The Background of IoT and Our Focus

The Internet of Things, a.k.a. IoT, is the network of physical devices, such as appliances, smartphones, vehicles, street lights, infrastructure elements, industrial machines, and so forth, which are also known as *things* (the T in IoT).

While working for The Procter & Gamble Company, Kevin Ashton coined the term *Internet of Things* (although he preferred the phrase Internet *for* Things).

© Anand Tamboli 2019
A. Tamboli, *Build Your Own IoT Platform*, https://doi.org/10.1007/978-1-4842-4498-2_1

At the outset, it was merely an exercise to identify physical objects, or things, with the help of RFID tags, and then using that information in software systems. Things have evolved since then. Several changes and ideas contributed to shaping the scope of IoT into something larger.

Today, IoT is a combination of physical objects that have some sort of computing power, some level of intelligence built into the object itself, media through which the object can be connected to the Internet ecosystem, and then the whole computing machinery of the Internet—going all the way to user devices and computers.

From the IoT platform perspective, our focus will be on where physical objects first meet the Internet and the magic that happens before software and applications take control.

These platforms are often termed as *middleware software* because they sit right in the middle of two heterogeneous things: physical objects and digital systems. Middleware is usually a mix of a high and a low level of logic, also incorporating the mixture of high- and low-level languages to accomplish the task.

You should be mindful of the fact that we are not going to build a full-blown, enterprise-grade IoT platform with all the bells and whistles. Instead, we will be agile and focus on reducing the time to market without breaking the bank. We will aim to design something that we can scale incrementally without having to do a lot of rework and potentially disrupting the current state of the work.

While there is no strict definition for what we can call an IoT platform, there is a general expectation that the platform will help high-level software, applications, and systems interact with lower-level protocols, methods of communication, and heterogeneous objects overall. This type of broad definition or understanding often means that there are far too many things that could fit in this criterion.

The IoT platform is one of the vital parts of an entire IoT ecosystem, and the term has become quite confusing due to marketing gimmicks and vendor proliferation.

How Many Platforms Are Out There?

Today, there are more than 500 platforms of various shapes and sizes, and this number will only keep growing. It is interesting to note that many of the platforms are losing their charm, so they are shutting down or merging with others. At the same time, a few platforms are morphing into more futuristic and powerful ones. In short, changes are happening in both directions.

An overview of these platforms shows that we can categorize all of them in three core types.

Platforms Supporting Network Servicing

These platforms support network servicing parts, such as MAC layer communication decoders and converters. These platforms essentially control and coordinate the telecommunications part of things. A good example is a network server for LoRaWAN communications. These platforms convert radio-level communication into raw data information and pass it on to upstream platforms or applications for further processing.

In addition to network service platforms, there are a few other parts, such as identity and key management services, and combinations of these.

Platforms Sitting Between Networks and Applications

These platforms support processing post network and pre-application, such as system-level protocol decoding, converting, decrypting, and so forth. These platforms can control and coordinate protocols and overall communication orchestration. They also support driver-level logic and the underlying architecture of the overall system that depends on them. We can treat them as the core plumbing of the system, which is what we will be building throughout this book.

Application-Layer Development Platforms

There are platforms that support high-level developments on the cloud. Most of these platforms help in the integration of multiple middleware platforms, other systems—such as ERPs and CRMs, and similar applications. The difference between this type of platform and the other two (network and middleware) is if the high-level platform fails, the other two will still function and may support parts of the high-level platform that are still working. On the contrary, if the network or middleware platform fails, there can be downtime for the overall system and solution.

Given that we have so many types of platforms and too many options available in the market, it is very important that we define what a good IoT middleware platform should have in it.

What Should a Good IoT Platform Have?

For every product, there are functions and features that are must-have or are nice to have. When we distinguish between the two, the answer is relatively simple. Building your own IoT platform makes much more sense. For any middleware platform to be worthy of being part of the Internet of Things, it is imperative that it has the following functionalities and capabilities.

- *Scalability*. Just like any new application or product, things start small and then grow later. Therefore, if the middleware platform must be at the core of the solution, it must be able to scale in the same proportion. It should not be a one-click change, which is okay; however, it should be reasonably easy to scale the platform without breaking existing functionalities and without disrupting existing production setup.

4

- *Reliability.* In general, it is an obvious expectation that anything that forms the core of a solution or product should be reliable. The level of redundancy built into the middleware slightly varies, depending on the end application, product, or industry vertical. For example, if the IoT platform is for medical devices, financial services, or security systems, the level of reliability expected is relatively high when compared to one for home appliances like coffee machine or similar others.

- *Customization.* Since we are building our own platform, it can be 100% customized; however, even if you were looking to buy off the shelf, customization without breaking the bank should be possible. If you cannot customize the middleware, then you have to modify your product or service to be fit for the platform, which is essentially working in the reverse direction.

- *Supported protocols and interfaces.* By fundamental definition, an IoT middleware platform sits between two heterogeneous systems: physical devices and cloud software (and there are umpteen numbers of device types and software). The platform should be able to coordinate with all of them, orchestrate things in unison, and speak all of the languages or protocols. Additionally, it needs the ability to create the required plugin and fill the gap whenever required, such that the middleware platform remains accommodating, for a very long time, before needing an overhaul.

- *Hardware agnostic.* The Internet of Things is essentially
  a group of heterogeneous connected things, hardware
  devices, computer systems, and software. This makes
  the requirement of being hardware-agnostic almost
  obvious. The reason why it still needs to be explicitly
  stated is due to a slightly skewed view. Many people
  think of hardware as an electronics circuit for a sensor,
  and for that view, we say that an IoT platform should be
  agnostic of whatever electronics you are using in your
  circuit. Whether it is an open source hardware design,
  proprietary circuit, or a mix, the platform should be
  able to support it.

- *Cloud agnostic.* Similar to being hardware agnostic,
  the platform also needs to be cloud agnostic. There are
  several cloud service providers—including Google,
  Microsoft, and Amazon Web Services (AWS)—but the
  platform should have no dependency on the cloud.
  Whether its your own service or a third-party cloud
  running behind a NAS (network-attached storage),
  the platform should be able to work. A good test of
  compliance is an answer to the question of whether
  the platform works on bare-metal servers. That is, if
  you get a virtual private server instance and install the
  platform, will it work? The answer should be a simple
  yes, which means the IoT platform is cloud agnostic.

- *Architecture and technology stack.* A well-defined
  architecture and the appropriate combination of the
  technology stack is a key thing that differentiates a good
  IoT platform from the others. The platform may be built
  on a rather weird combination of technologies that are
  not known for working together nicely. Maybe

the technology used is going to be deprecated in next few years, especially during the operational timespan of your usage. If this is the case, you should stay away from it. The same goes for the architecture, or the so-called "plumbing" of the middleware. If the architecture is not flexible enough for future changes, that is a red flag. A completely fluid architecture is not a good fit either. You need a good combination of a fluid and a rigid architecture backed by a solid, efficient technology stack.

- *Security.* Over the last several years, the Internet of Things has become a laughing stock, mainly due to poorly managed security aspects in far too many applications and IoT solutions. The saying, "The S in IoT stands for security," has become commonplace and is a strong indication that security in a middleware platform is as important as it is in other aspects of the IoT ecosystem. Security becomes a vital consideration factor if you choose a multitenant platform. The multitenant aspect makes the system more vulnerable, because your own application may be just fine but another application using the same platform (a co-tenant of your application) can create security problems for every other tenant; the risk is always present.

- *Cost.* The budget set for an IoT platform has a relatively larger influence on cost factors; however, overall, if the cost of the platform (whether it was built in-house or bought off the shelf) does not justify the functionality and features, then it must be reviewed. In short, the platform should add enough value to justify its cost.

- *Support.* As much as ongoing support for platform management is essential, there is also support required for solution integration purposes. And as a mandatory requirement, the middleware platform should have strong support in the design, development, deployment, and management of the solution on an ongoing basis.

Why Should You Build Your Own IoT Platform?

As businesses and working scenarios evolve, we see many smaller companies delving into the IoT. However, not having your own IoT platform is one of the impediments or roadblocks for such an evolution.

Why not use a freemium or free trial platform? What lies ahead is a greater challenge when things scale and costs skyrocket exponentially. When the trial expires or a freemium is not enough, users find themselves locked in. This is challenging for many small players. Having your own IoT platform is a much better solution.

Buying off the shelf or a freemium might seem like better choices at the outset, however, there is a trade-off. IoT platforms that save you time may cost more in the end, depending on how vendors price them. This is mainly because the charges are either use-based or device-based. In addition, a subscription fee can add up over time. Yet, you get the benefit of significantly lower up-front costs, which means no capital expenditures; however, it also depends on how you plan to charge the end users or customers who buy your IoT product or solution.

IoT platforms that are initially inexpensive will likely cost you in time. This comes back to the same point: the less you spend, the more work you have to do on your own to integrate and nurse the platforms. If you must spend a significant amount of time, it would be better spent on building your own, don't you think?

Building your own also supports the idea of being frugal at the start and then investing only when and where necessary. This would help you to tap into technology advancements without bank-breaking budgets. More importantly, you can get off the ground very quickly. This book explains how to build an IoT platform within 24 hours, which is contrary to the longer times required to adapt into off-the-shelf or full-feature platforms, and learn how to use free trial or freemium platforms.

If having full control means a lot to you, then definitely build your own solution. Buying an off-the-shelf solution often means that you subordinate your requirements and retrofit your solution to suit what is available. This means that you could be building a subpar solution, if not an outright bad one. Building your own platform gives you full flexibility and control over what you want, including how and when you build it.

Building your own from the scratch is always a fulfilling learning experience, and it should not be missed, if possible.

Summary

This chapter gave you a very brief background on IoT and our area of focus in this book. We discussed the types of platforms that are in play and which characteristics a good IoT platform should have. With some more rationale behind why building your own platform is a good choice, let's dive into further reading. In the next chapter, we look at the building blocks of an IoT solution and learn more about the solution ecosystem.

CHAPTER 2

The Building Blocks of an IoT Solution

The overall hype around IoT has unexpectedly hindered the understanding of how it works. If you ask 20 people about how it works, you will get 20 answers. Most of those answers would cover how outcomes of IoT or manifested IoT solutions work; not the way IoT works. There is a lot of technology under the hood that makes IoT possible.

In this chapter, I discuss the following:

- The key building blocks of an IoT solution

- A detailed block diagram of an IoT platform

- How blocks work together in a meaningful way

- A proposed approach for building our platform

These topics will help us identify how it all works, and then we can plan the building of our IoT platform in an effective way.

Let's first discuss some of the various terminologies, which are often used interchangeably. There is a difference between an *IoT solution* and an *IoT application.* An IoT solution usually means an end-to-end product, service, or a mix of both; whereas an IoT application usually refers to IT software or a mobile application, or a combination of both. Clearly, IoT solutions encompass many more things than an IoT application. A lot of business context, customer context, and geopolitical context influence IoT solutions.

© Anand Tamboli 2019
A. Tamboli, *Build Your Own IoT Platform*, https://doi.org/10.1007/978-1-4842-4498-2_2

However, from an IoT platform perspective, it sits on the edge of IoT applications and is usually a borderline system to deal with physical objects—a.k.a. things and software systems. A block diagram of a typical IoT solution is shown in Figure 2-1, which represents IoT solutions architecture in a manner that distinctively shows the building blocks separated by the important aspects of a larger system.

The Functional Blocks of an IoT Solution

At a high level, we can identify IoT solutions comprising four major functional blocks. If any of these blocks are missing, then it is not prudent to call it an IoT solution.

Devices (a.k.a. "things") are physical sensors and actuators. They measure various parameters and translate them into electrical or digital data. These sensors are either connected to the host devices (typical for legacy upgrades) or integrated into the host devices (modern). These devices are critical nodes of an IoT application and are required to deliver full-solution functionality by acting as inputs, outputs, or both. Typical examples of such devices are thermostats, intelligent mousetraps, connected refrigerators, and so forth.

Gateways are edge devices that can communicate with the upstream system in one of two ways: with or without a gateway. Some devices have the capability to communicate directly over Internet Protocol (IP) using various communication protocols, such as REST, MQTT, AMQP, CoAP, and so forth. These capabilities are usually a result of integrated communication modules, such as Wi-Fi or GSM chips, which enable a device to connect to network gateways, such as Wi-Fi routers and mobile towers, and communicate with the upstream layer directly. In these cases, routers and mobile towers perform the job of the gateway.

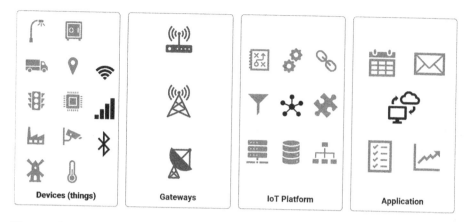

Figure 2-1. *Functional blocks of an IoT solution*

However, not all devices are capable of direct Internet connectivity and do not have the necessary hardware built in. In these cases, they need to piggyback on some other device to help their data get pushed to the upstream layer. Gateways help devices do this. Usually, hardware gateways are built with dual communication technologies, which enable them to communicate with downstream devices with one type of channel and with upstream layers with another type of channel. Typical examples of such gateway capabilities include GSM and RF, GSM and Bluetooth, Wi-Fi and Bluetooth, Wi-Fi and XBee, LoRaWAN and Ethernet, and so forth. In some cases, smartphones are used as gateways, which is more prominent with Bluetooth Low Energy (BLE) devices.

In addition to providing a transport mechanism, a gateway can also provide optional functions, such as data segregation, clean up, aggregation, deduplication, and edge computing.

An *IoT platform* is the orchestrator of the whole IoT solution and is often hosted in the cloud. This block is responsible for communicating with downstream devices and ingesting large amounts of data at a very high speed. The platform is also responsible for storage of the data in a time series and structured format for further processing and analysis.

Depending upon the sophistication built into it, a platform may support deep data analyses and other operations. However, the core of the IoT platform is as an orchestrator of the whole system.

In most scenarios, *applications* are the front face of the whole solution; it must be presented to the end user in a meaningful way. These applications are desktop based, mobile based, or both. Applications also enrich the data from the platform in various ways and present it to the users in a usable format. Additionally, these applications integrate with other systems and applications at the interface level and enable interapplication data exchange. A typical example of such an operation is inventory-tracking devices equipped with tracking mobile applications to the users, and the data fed to the ERP system for stock keeping.

The Detailed Block Diagram of an IoT Platform

We are more interested in the mechanics of the third block: the IoT platform. Let's look at all the fundamental inclusions that an IoT platform should have to perform effectively. Figure 2-2 shows the block diagram of a typical IoT platform.

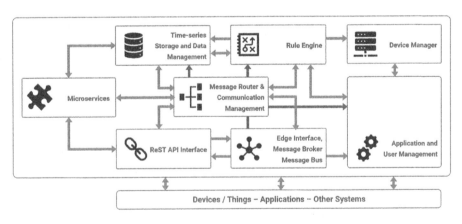

Figure 2-2. *Block diagram of a typical IoT platform*

Interconnecting arrows indicate the data and information flow between each block. Each block is indicative of the major functional component of the platform. The platform is installed on a virtual cloud machine or VPS (virtual private server). It is highly recommended to use a Linux-based operating system, such as Ubuntu, Centos, Debian, OpenWRT, or LEDE, for better performance, security features, and overall control of the platform. The concept and block-level architecture does not change for any of these operating systems.

Edge Interface, Message Broker, and Message Bus

This module deals and talks with the physical world, especially heterogeneous devices and sensors. Since devices could be communicating over a multitude of communication technologies, such as Wi-Fi, Bluetooth, LoRaWAN, GPRS, and so forth, this module needs to cater to all of them. We can achieve this in a modular format where each type of communication protocol is dealt with separately. As an example, a Wi-Fi-capable device can be a REST API, which caters to the constrained devices. It could be an MQTT-based message broker, which enables communication in a pub/sub manner. For LoRaWAN (Long Range Wide Area Network)–based devices, there is another plugin to the main message broker, which talks with LoRaWAN network servers and performs decoding of packets.

Note   Pub-sub refers to the publish-and-subscribe paradigm of communication. It is explained in Chapter 6.

This module decouples the entire platform from devices in an effective way. Many edge interfaces and protocols are supported for modern IoT devices. Regardless of the medium of communication, network type used, and protocols in play, the message broker's job is to consolidate the data in a unified manner and push it to the common message bus. All the other functional blocks share this message bus for further operation. The broker acts as a coordinator and consolidator of messages.

Message Router and Communication Management

Once the messages are available on the main message bus, the message may need to include more context or refinement to be useful to other modules. Some messages need feature enrichment and additional information to be appended or added separately, which depends on the context of the device deployment and application requirements. The functionality of enriching existing data messages, rebroadcasting them to the message bus, publishing additional contextual information and other messages after the main message arrives, and tagging them as appropriate is the job of the communication management module. Communication management functions coordinate with the message broker and the rule engine block and interacts with the device manager, as required.

In addition, the communication management module performs the duties of format conversions; for example, it translates data from CSV to JSON, or binary to text format, and so forth. We can also task it to perform certain operations, like deduplication of messages. Deduplication is the process of eliminating or discarding multiple duplicate messages or redundant data packets from the devices, as they may not be of any use. Deduplication schemes are dependent on device or sensor types, and we need to implement them on a case-by-case basis, although the methodology remains the same. As a communications router, this module can control further messaging and communication on the platform.

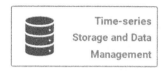

Time-Series Storage and Data Management

As the name suggests, this block stores all the received and parsed data that is available on the message bus in sequential (i.e., time-series style). While data storage is not the core function of the IoT platform, modules outside the platform handle it; although, it is an essential activity for coordination and orchestration perspective. Very often, communication and routing modules, or the message broker itself, need recent data for specific functional purposes; this storage comes in handy for all such instances.

For many IoT applications, users prefer to extract the data away from the IoT platform and store it in an application data warehouse for further processing. Therefore, it is often utilized for interim storage of the device data and is not meant for large-sized dataset storage.

Rule Engine

In my view, this is a very powerful block and provides enhanced capabilities to the platform. The rule engine is the execution block that monitors the message bus and events across the platform and takes action based on set rules.

For example, a typical rule engine function may look like this: "Trigger and broadcast alert message when the downstream device sends a data packet containing the keyword ka-boom." The rule engine is constantly listening to the message bus broadcasts. When the communication block puts up a decoded data packet from the downstream device on to the message bus, a rule triggers. The rule engine broadcasts another message (alert) to the message bus. Since this happens all within the IoT platform and among closely coordinated modules, execution speed is quite fast.

The rule engine also helps with building modular rules for decoding and enriching existing or received data from devices, and therefore, augments the communication module's functionality. In addition to that, it is easy to implement callbacks to other modules, applications, programs, and systems.

The REST API Interface

Restful APIs are useful for support functions and utilities that do not need constant or real-time connectivity and access. Although typically used by upstream programs and applications, downstream devices can also access these APIs when needed.

A classic example of such a use case is a temperature sensor with Wi-Fi____33 connectivity that sends readings every 15 minutes. Due to such a long time between two subsequent readings, a real-time connection or an always-on connectivity is undesired. A simple HTTP operation can do the data-sending job relatively more efficiently. In this case, the sensor can send the data over REST API to the platform. The REST API works with the message broker and communications manager to present the received data post to the main message bus; it may also use time-series database records to send back the response to the sensor. This response may contain additional information for the sensor to do its job in a certain way for the next round.

This API block can also support data aggregation and bulk operational functionalities, such as querying multiple records by the upstream application. This way, upstream applications and systems remain decoupled from the core platform blocks, thereby maintaining the partition of functions and ensuring security. Various role-based authentications can be built in for access to the API.

The REST API block can also feed into the rule engine and allow applications to configure or trigger specific rules at any given point in time. This also makes it possible for downstream devices to utilize the same functionality, which could be handy when devices need to initiate certain workflows automatically in place of application triggers. A good example is a smart lock; for instance, when there is activity at the front door that needs the homeowner's attention when she is away from home. An upstream application may notify the user when the smart lock reports activity, and then expects the user to respond or react for further steps. If the user is not available, then the application can trigger the rule for predefined actions. If the severity of the alert is relatively high, then the device may be configured to not wait for user action or response, but directly trigger the default workflow (e.g., notifying security, etc.). These functionalities can come in handy when designing and operating an autonomous and intelligent fleet of devices.

Microservices

Besides data management, manipulation, and exchange functionalities, the IoT platform also needs certain support functions to function effectively. Services such as text messaging or email notifications, verifications, captcha, social media authentications, or payment services integration are a few examples of these auxiliary services. These services are bundled in the microservices block.

In case of frequent use of certain functionalities within the platform, it can be bundled and packaged under this block to separate it from the mainstream platform. Once separated and packaged, it then can be exposed to the blocks within and outside the platform for reuse.

Device Manager

When the platform starts to host approximately 50 or more devices, things could become difficult to manage. It becomes necessary to have some type of central control in place for managing things (a.k.a. devices). This is where the device manager block helps. It essentially provides the generic functionality of managing devices as assets. This includes listing all the devices, their active-inactive status, battery levels, network conditions, access keys, readings, stored data access, device details, session information, and other similar things.

The device manager also helps with managing over-the-air updates for a fleet of devices, or central monitoring functions for system admins. In certain use cases, devices also need access rights, and users may be assigned certain access rights to a set of devices. Management of such an accessibility matrix becomes easy with the device manager.

Application and User Management

This block provides functionalities similar to the device manager. The difference is that it provides functionalities for upstream applications and users. Typical user management functions, such as passwords and credentials, access keys, logins, and rights are managed through this block. For upstream applications and various other integrated systems, API keys, credentials, and access can be managed through the same block.

While it may appear to be more of an application-level functionality, it remains in an IoT platform's interest to bind it as a platform function, so that it is integrated tightly with the overall architecture and set of things. IoT is the system of systems, and heterogeneous systems are a fact of this phenomenon. Letting these system functions get out of sync is the last thing that you want to happen with IoT solutions.

Is Everything from this Block Architecture Mandatory?

No. While eight of the blocks define a very well-architected IoT platform, not all of them are mandatory or necessary. A specific use case or industry vertical may define this situation differently. You may not need all blocks at the outset, and they may be added later in the life cycle of the platform development.

The core functional blocks—the device interface and message broker, the message router and communications module, data storage, device management, and the rule engine are critical for the effective functioning of an IoT platform. Other blocks—REST APIs, microservices, and application and user management—are good to have and often make life easy but are not mandatory and do not obstruct functionality of the IoT platform.

When developing our IoT platform from the ground up, we will keep these functionalities on the back burner and will only implement them if time permits and resources are available.

What Is the Proposed Approach?

To develop an IoT platform in the quickest amount of time, we will not only develop it in modular form but will also do it in an agile way. Each module will be planned with functions and features set out, developed, and then deployed on the cloud for testing. Once we test an individual module and find it to be working as expected, we can go to the next module.

As a first step, we will set up the cloud environment for the platform. This is followed by setting up the essential components to develop for our first module: the edge interface and the message broker. The logical next step is to set up time-series data storage. Then we will develop basic REST APIs for the platform, followed by message router functionality.

Some of the microservices are developed after we have set up a fundamental wireframe of the platform. We will then iterate through all of these blocks a few more times to make a stable core for the platform.

Once we are happy with the core functionalities, the rule engine can be set up, followed by the device management functions. Application and user management is reviewed at the end because it is among the non-essential modules.

Summary

In this chapter, we discussed the functional blocks of an IoT platform, and we decided on the approach that we want to take toward building our own platform. In the next chapter, we discuss the essential requirements for building a platform. The detailed specifications of required elements, and how and where to get them, are covered. Chapter 3 also expands on the functional block diagram of platforms in the context of our planned work.

CHAPTER 3

The Essentials for Building Your Own Platform

Before we start the core activity of building the platform, it is important to lay down a solid foundation. This will not only keep our platform scalable and solid in the long run, but it will also help us to clearly articulate current and future technical requirements. In this chapter, we will

- Choose the operating system for our cloud instance
- List the base specifications of the instance
- Determine what we need on our local computers for access
- Expand on our own IoT platform's block diagram

Deciding Cloud Instance Specifics

To build our own platform, at the very least, we need a bare-metal cloud instance. While there are a few options for operating systems in such instances, the most preferred option is a Linux-based OS. Let's look at what makes it the preferred option.

© Anand Tamboli 2019
A. Tamboli, *Build Your Own IoT Platform*, https://doi.org/10.1007/978-1-4842-4498-2_3

- *The total cost of ownership.* The most obvious advantage is that Linux is free, whereas Windows is not. A single-user license may not cost much; however, the total cost of ownership can be higher over time, and thus increase ongoing costs.

- *Reliability.* Linux-based systems are more reliable than Windows. Traditionally, Linux systems are known to run for years without having a failure or a situation that demands restarting. This is a critical criterion for the selection of an operating system for our IoT platform.

- *Hardware resources.* Linux systems consume fewer system resources like RAM, disk space, and so forth, when compared to Windows. For our IoT platform, we need at least 1 GB of RAM and 20–25 GB of disk space. That said, costs remain in control if we go with a Linux-based system. A Windows system may not run efficiently with this level of specification.

- *Security.* Linux-based systems are built with security at a fundamental level. It is the choice for more secure environments. Due to this inherent security, we will save on antivirus costs and additional system overhead.

- *Control.* Control is one of the main reasons for building your own IoT platform. Linux-based systems provide control at all levels. No bloatware means a lot for speedy systems like our platform. Being in control of what is installed helps us closely maintain that control.

- *Power.* Windows presently runs only equipment that will not run at the low power desired for systems running often or always.

Additional Specifications

We need a minimum of 1 GB RAM and at least 20–25 GB of disk space on the operating system for effective basic functioning. We also need Node.js and Node-RED software for writing our platform code.

With a Linux-based system, we need a LAMP stack installed on our system. A LAMP stack is a set of open source software for creating websites and web applications. LAMP is an acronym for Linux-Apache-MySQL-PHP. It consists of the Linux operating system, Apache HTTP Server, the MySQL relational database management system, and the PHP programming language.

In addition to these basic software packages, we need several add-ons; we will get to that list as we progress. Once we have our instance up and running with the LAMP stack, Node.js, and Node-RED installed, we have a basic infrastructure ready to proceed.

Where Do We Get this Cloud Instance?

There are quite a few choices for putting a cloud instance on a virtual private server—AWS (Amazon Web Services), Google Cloud, Alibaba Cloud, and DigitalOcean, to name a few. Moreover, there could be many more, which may spring up soon.

Which vendor you choose for the cloud instance depends on your vendor preferences, pricing for the instance offered by these vendors, and many other factors.

On many fronts, DigitalOcean seems to be a good choice; mainly because it offers a nice, clear user interface without the unnecessary clutter of choices and options. This is the key to remaining agile and finishing tasks quickly.

From an affordability perspective, DigitalOcean is clearly the best option given that it has transparent pricing, as compared to complex millisecond calculations from other vendors. The price is based on hourly billing, and it is usually fixed for a month on monthly usage.

DigitalOcean is not a managed service like AWS or Google Cloud, but that should be okay for our purpose. A cloud instance on DigitalOcean servers must be managed by the owners—from upgrades to patches, and so forth, which is not the case for AWS and Google Cloud. However, when dealing with bare-metal cloud instances, things are not that simple, so even with Google Cloud and AWS, you have to take care of your own system if it is a bare-metal instance.

In short, if you have a massive scale implementation, AWS or Google Cloud should be chosen; for all other purposes, DigitalOcean is a better choice.

For our platform, we want agility (i.e., build within 24 hours), cost-effectiveness, transparency in billing, full control, and other such aspects. So, we will use DigitalOcean as our cloud instance in this book. However, if you are comfortable with other vendors, that is fine.

What About Our Own Machine?

Although we will be doing most things in a cloud instance, and the majority of the development will happen in a cloud environment, we still need some tools installed on our local machine (laptop or desktop).

At the outset, we need at least three tools/software.

- *Terminal emulator for SSH.* We will use a program called PuTTY, which is a well-known and widely used terminal emulator. It is a free and open source program with support for several network protocols, including SSH, SCP, Telnet, and so forth. It allows raw socket connections. It can also connect to a serial port of a computer, which may come in handy when testing a few hardware modules on our platform.

- *Basic editor.* This can be as basic as a Notepad program. I recommend Notepad++. It is a free software text editor for use with Microsoft Windows. It supports working with multiple open files in a single window and thus comes in very handy. The project's name comes from the C increment operator.

- *FTP program.* There are several choices for FTP applications, including WinSCP, FileZilla, CoreFTP, and FireFTP. We will use FileZilla throughout this book.

PuTTY, Notepad++, and FileZilla are effective and fit for our purposes; however, they are not mandatory. You are free to choose any other available options.

Expanding on the IoT Platform Block Diagram

In Chapter 2, we discussed a detailed block diagram of an IoT platform. Now we will decide which blocks we want to prioritize for quick development and which functions/features we want to develop in the first pass.

Edge Interface, Message Broker, and Message Bus

This will be a fundamental function for our IoT platform, and we will work on it at the very beginning. We will use the MQTT protocol for message exchange because MQTT is almost a de facto protocol for edge devices and IoT applications communication. We will discuss MQTT later. This will be one of the most critical modules of our IoT platform.

Message Router and Communications Management

At the outset, we will develop only a skeletal message router. It will not have a major communications management functionality. We will develop this module as a placeholder for the second pass of the development.

Time-Series Storage and Data Management

As explained in the previous chapter, this is not a core function; however, it is one of the elements that we will build in the first pass to use later.

REST API Interface

To test the platform functionality from device to platform and from web applications to platform, the REST API is necessary. We will start with skeletal APIs, and then add complex features in later passes.

Microservices

Although we will not be developing them until the second pass, we will be making a few arrangements to make sure that when we add them in the later stage, we will not have to make major changes to the fundamental design. By design, microservices are not critical in an IoT platform.

Rule Engine

As this is one of the most powerful features in an IoT platform, we will keep it in perspective from the beginning. The rule engine cannot be developed in one go. We need multiple passes to make it good.

Device Manager and Application Manager

While good to have, these functionalities are not a core part of the platform, so we will not be developing them for our IoT platform. It is still easy to use numerous devices and applications without formally having a device manager and an application manager.

Our Own IoT Platform Block Diagram

Now that we have listed our focus areas for development, the revised IoT platform block diagram would look something like Figure 3-1.

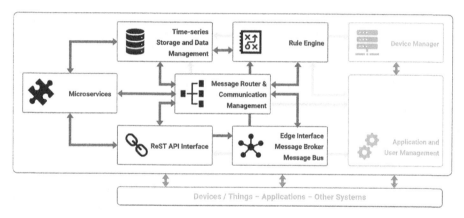

Figure 3-1. *Block diagram of our planned IoT platform implementation*

In a nutshell, our platform will be fully functional from the perspective of a core IoT platform. All the aspects that are considered *features* will be left out for future enhancements. This is a good compromise of speed over features and will in no way harm the product performance of this platform.

Summary

So far, we have made various choices for cloud instance specifications. We listed what is needed on our laptops to build the platform.

As a next step, we will create a wish list for our IoT platform's REST API, and we will detail what we want each API to do. We will also list the requirements for an edge interface and broker, a database manager, the message router, and a few microservices.

CHAPTER 4

Let's Create Our Platform Wish List

Although it may be easier to work as we go, having the requirements defined in advance (as many as possible) will help us create the required platform fabric faster and more efficiently.

In this chapter, we list the expectations and general requirements for each module in our IoT platform. We discuss the following:

- How we (and *things*) connect with the platform in real time

- How we want to store the data

- The types of APIs that we will build

- The microservices and utilities the we need to build

Connecting with the Platform in Real Time

One of the challenges faced by web applications is the ability to communicate in real time. While synchronous communication is quite common, and we can achieve that with typical HTTP-like requests, being able to communicate asynchronously is not effectively possible with the same format and technique. However, connecting and communicating with the IoT platform in real time is the key requirement for IoT solutions

© Anand Tamboli 2019
A. Tamboli, *Build Your Own IoT Platform*, https://doi.org/10.1007/978-1-4842-4498-2_4

and applications. This is where we need to use a message broker and implement a publish-subscribe-like mechanism.

This is a key reason why message brokers are important components of the latest web technologies. Message brokers are generally middleware programs that provide asynchronous communication abilities to all connected applications and devices, with the help of a publish-subscribe mechanism.

The publish-subscribe mechanism is an interesting paradigm, as it does not make it necessary for either of the parties to be online at the same time. Moreover, it also makes it possible that any party can initiate the data transfer regardless of whether the other party is ready for it. This is totally opposite to what HTTP does, where the client must originate the request to which the server will respond. The server cannot contact the client in real time. When we connect the server and client with the publish-subscribe mechanism through a message broker, either of them can send data, which is a powerful functionality.

So, in short, we need a message broker program.

It is important that the message broker we select fulfill certain essential criterion. In general, two criterions are important: easy to configure and maintain, and stable enough for the production environment.

Using MQTT as the Message Broker

While there could be several techniques for message broking, we will use the MQTT standard, as this is almost the de facto standard protocol for IoT applications and solutions.

MQTT stands for MQ Telemetry Transport. It is a publish-subscribe, extremely simple and lightweight messaging protocol designed for constrained devices and low-bandwidth, high-latency, or unreliable networks. The design principles are to minimize network bandwidth and device resource requirements while attempting to ensure reliability and assurance of delivery. These principles make the protocol ideal for the emerging machine-to-machine (M2M) or Internet of Things world of connected devices, and for mobile applications, where bandwidth and battery power are at a premium.(mqtt.org, 2013)

There are many implementations of MQTT—commercially available and open source. Mosquitto is a popular open source MQTT implementation, and we will use it to build our message broker. We can implement a message broker with any other Node.js implementation of MQTT, and it is still open source. Let's explore that option later, as it might be useful as a fallback secondary broker for our platform's redundancy.

How Do We Want to Store the Data?

So far, we have decided to use Mosquitto as our MQTT message broker. Brokers are not storage providers, however. They are more like a message courier or conduit through which messages or data pass through. This data is ephemeral, and if not stored, cannot be seen or retrieved later.

From a platform's perspective, we need this storage and retrieval mechanism so that we are able to retrieve data later; and for non-synchronized applications and devices, this data can serve as a shadow copy of the information.

Since we are building our platform on an Ubuntu server with LAMP stack, MySQL is the default and obvious choice. Not only this, MySQL consistently ranks as the second-most popular database according to DB-Engines Ranking in 2018.

The key question is how we want to store the data. The data that we refer to is transactional data that passes through our message broker and central message bus communication manager. This data has only a few information fields, which are used for data processing and audit purposes, and accordingly, our data storage schema has to be suitable for that.

With MQTT communication, a data packet comes with two fields in each message: topic and payload. The topic typically works as a key for the data, while the payload is actual data or content. Since MQTT is a messaging protocol and does not necessarily specify the format of the payload, we can be flexible. However, to maintain scalability and a unified approach throughout the platform, we will use JSON (JavaScript Object Notation) encoding for our payload (a.k.a. data packet) throughout the platform. This will not only help us in maintaining consistency, but it will also make our platform extensible and easily adaptable to new changes.

Data Storage Schema

JSON data essentially is an ASCII character string and is the topic in the MQTT message. It is important to note that MQTT also supports binary data packets, which can have non-ASCII characters too. This means that we can easily transmit binary files and data through the message broker, and we should keep this in mind when designing our platform.

Besides storing topic and related data payloads, we also need to assign a unique ID for each message stored. In addition, most importantly, since this is going to be a time-series database, we need store timestamps for each message. Apart from these fields, we do not need any other information to be stored in the core of the IoT platform at this stage. With these considerations, our database table schema is shown in Figure 4-1.

Sr	Name	Type	Null	Extra
1	ID	int (11)	No	AUTO_INCREMENT
2	Topic	varchar (1024)	No	
3	Payload	varchar (2048)	No	
4	Timestamp	varchar (15)	No	

Figure 4-1. Time-series data storage table schema

The following briefly explains each column.

- *ID*. The incremental unique number. We are using the MySQL autoincrement feature for this.

- *Topic*. Declared as a varchar to allow us to store a variable length of data in this field. A topic can be any length, and depending upon the application, it changes. We will keep a 1 KB restriction, which is big enough for any conceivable topic name.

- *Payload*. The data packet is a larger size and can be any length (hence, variable type). However, we will restrict the payload packet storage to 2 KB for now. Keep in mind that these are configurable options for MySQL and thus can be changed without affecting the application. We can increase the size and limit without affecting previously stored data; however, when lowering the size, prior data may be truncated. This can be decided as needed.

- *Timestamp*. We will store UNIX (a.k.a. epoch-based timestamps), which are UNIX-style, date-time stamps represented in integer format. The epoch (or UNIX time, POSIX time, or UNIX timestamp) is the number of seconds that have elapsed since January 1, 1970 (midnight UTC/GMT), and this does not account for leap seconds. This may not be a precise timestamp but close enough for real-life scenarios, which is enough for our application purposes.

Based on this table structure, we will store every data packet received in the Payload column and store its topic in the Topic column; both stored in as-is format. The timestamp will be from our platform system time, and the ID will be automatically incremented. This will enable us to query data when needed in the same sequence that it was stored and with reference to the timestamp—making it a time-series dataset.

Accessing Platform Resources Through APIs

With the Mosquitto MQTT broker and the time-series storage in place, our platform will be able to ingest data packets and communicate over MQTT in general. This communication (over MQTT) will be data stream–based and will not necessarily have any built-in intelligence without the rest of the platform.

Devices or applications that are connected to the stream are able to access the data in real time; however, when offline or not connected, there is no mechanism to ask for data. This is where our APIs will play an important role.

In the computer programming domain, API means *application programming interface*, which is a set of subroutines or subprocedure definitions, communication protocols, and tools for building software.

Note   In general, it is a set of clearly defined methods of communication among various components (of a computer program or system). A good API makes it easier to develop a computer program by providing all the building blocks, which the programmer can put together for a meaningful purpose.

Let's categorize our APIs into four different types. This will help us keep the development modular and pluggable.

- *Data access APIs*. These APIs help us access time-series data storage in our IoT platform and manipulate it in a limited manner. Additionally, this API helps create linkages between live data streams (MQTT based) and non-live data streams (HTTP based).

- *Utility APIs.* There are certain utilities that could be required on a non-regular basis for many applications. A classic example of these utilities is data conversion or transformation in a certain format. If an application or device needs to encode or encrypt the data for one-off uses, or needs to translate or transform it for a specific condition, then it can utilize some of these APIs. Essentially, they are packed functions shared by multiple resources across and outside the platform.

- *Microservice APIs.* Endpoints that are functionality based or serve a very specific and predefined purpose form part of this group. These are typically application services such as email and text messaging.

- *Plug-in APIs.* Some of the interfaces that we will build will patch up two sections of the platform, which otherwise are not connected. Some of these APIs also act as a front end to mobile or computer applications.

Data Accessing APIs

To access time-series data safely and appropriately, we will design a set of APIs to cater to various scenarios and requirements. In general, we need at least seven endpoints.

> **Note**   Each requirement is numbered so that we can easily refer to
> them throughout the book. Data requirements start with a D, while
> microservice and utility requirements start with an M.

- *D1. Get a single data record.* Enables applications and
  devices to query a single data record from the time-
  series data storage based on the specified topic or topic
  pattern.

- *D2. Get several data records in series.* Enables
  applications and devices to query multiple data records
  based on a specified topic or topic pattern.

- *D3. Get one or several records based on certain
  condition(s).* Enables applications to query one or more
  data records based on a specified condition—for topic
  or payload, or both. The condition could be a topic or
  payload pattern, or timestamp dependent, such as data
  within a time period.

- *D4. Store data record sent over an API (if not sent over
  MQTT stream).* In addition to querying data from
  time-series storage, we want applications and devices
  to store the data in the time-series store. This is useful
  for devices and applications that cannot communicate
  over a live MQTT data stream.

- *D5. Delete a single data record.* Enables applications
  or devices to delete a single data record based on the
  specified topic. Note that we do not want to implement
  the topic pattern mechanism because of accidental
  data purges.

- *D6. Delete several data records in series.* Deletes a set of data records from the dataset based on topic. It is useful if we want to keep data storage lean and light in weight. A typical scenario for this requirement is removing all the data after 24 hours, or combining it with a multirecord query, getting the data out of platform storage and storing it somewhere for audit or regulatory purposes.

- *D7. Delete one or several records based on certain condition(s).* Like querying one or multiple data records based on a specified condition, we may need to delete them from the time-series storage. Although this is a useful functionality, it needs a built-in level of safety, which we will discuss in detail.

Elementary Microservices and Utilities

Here we list some of the microservices and utilities that we want to use on our IoT platform, frequently but not regularly.

- *M1. Publish current timestamp.* This service is something I highly recommend for distributed applications. Often, we find that the systems are not coordinated due to time zone differences and system clock limitations. We can overcome this with the help of a time broadcasting service. The other alternative for this is the use of NTP (Network Time Protocol); however, not all the applications or devices have access to NTP servers, which limits their ability to time synchronize operations.

We will use this utility to publish/broadcast time values from our own IoT platform, so that all systems are synchronized with our platform. We can synchronize the platform with NTP servers separately; regardless, there is a stable reference source in the form of our platform.

- *M2. Get current timestamp.* This is a polling service of the publish current timestamp function. This service is helpful when a device or application wants to poll and wants to know the current timestamp if it missed a prior broadcast and cannot wait until the next broadcast; or in case the device or application is forced to synchronize by the user or a business rule.

- *M3. Get unique or random number/string.* This is a very handy service for random strings and number generation and usage. We can use randomly generated numbers and strings for creating unique keys or reference numbers. We can also use them as random passwords or as tokens.

- *M4. Get UUID.* A UUID (Universal Unique Identifier) is like a random number or string generation service, but a bit more structured and universally unique. A UUID algorithm is guaranteed to be different or it is extremely likely to be different from any other UUIDs generated until the year 3400 (i.e., 1500 years from now). Similar to random strings, we can use UUIDs for generating keys or passwords for devices and applications.

- *M5. Send an email.* A ubiquitous and probably frequently used service by several applications and platforms. We need an email service for automation,

alerts, user checks, and verifications; password resets;
key communications; and more. This is a must-have
service in our IoT platform.

- *M6. Send a text message.* We can use text messages
  for purposes similar to email. Additionally, we can
  use it for implementing two-factor authentication for
  our systems or critical sections where an additional
  security layer is required. Our applications and other
  applications connected to the platform can use this
  service.

- *M7. MQTT callback registration.* Because the MQTT
  data feed is live, for applications that depend on an
  HTTP-only mechanism, there is no way to be notified
  of newly available data unless the application is polling
  continuously or frequently. To avoid this, we develop
  a service that essentially creates a webhook to use
  whenever the platform receives a data packet matching
  given topic or payload criterion. This way, HTTP-only
  applications can post or transmit the data packet using
  the REST API (as in D4) and receive it (be notified) with
  this service. We may have to leverage the rules engine
  for writing this service. Note that this applies only to
  server-based applications; hardware devices are not
  likely getting any benefit from the callback.

Routing and Filtering Data and Messages

Routing and filtering data flow and messages are going to be only a general
architecture, and will not be final at the first stage. We will keep it evolving
based on additions of new devices and applications.

Updated Block Diagram of Our IoT Platform

Remember that none of the requirements that we have listed are hard and fast. Many of them could be built later, or skipped altogether. So far, we have defined the base requirements for four of the major blocks of the platform.

The agile way that we are building our platform enables us to add more features and functionalities in any of these modules. This way, we can get our core functional IoT platform up and running in less than 24 hours, and then keep augmenting it on an ongoing basis. The updated block diagram of our IoT platform is shown in Figure 4-2.

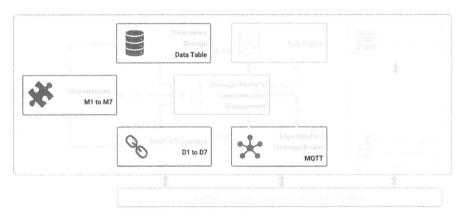

Figure 4-2. *Updated block diagram of our IoT platform*

Summary

In this chapter, we made a few key decisions related to the data storage schema and real-time connectivity. We also defined our API, microservice, and utility requirements. Now we hit the road and start building something.

The next chapter is completely hands-on. Accordingly, you may want to ensure that you have a laptop computer with all the software utilities installed. We also require a fully qualified domain name for our platform. It would be a good idea to think about this and select one.

CHAPTER 5

Here We Go!

With the wish list of requirements and a detailed understanding of the block-level architecture of our IoT platform, it is time to kick off the work.

In this chapter, we will

- Initialize our cloud instance

- Install basic and advanced software stacks, as required

- Add security profiles to the fundamental stack

- Create and configure a time-series database

- Give our platform a domain name

This is the longest chapter in the book and a very important one too. To make the most of it, I recommend that you read through the whole chapter first, and then jump into the hands-on implementation in the second round. This way, if anything is missing or needed, you will not be stuck in the middle of the implementation.

Initializing the Cloud Instance

This is the very first step in building our platform. I suggest that you have handy every prerequisite discussed in the previous chapter.

© Anand Tamboli 2019

A. Tamboli, *Build Your Own IoT Platform*, https://doi.org/10.1007/978-1-4842-4498-2_5

Register and Create

First, we register and initialize an instance on DigitalOcean, and then install the base software stack. Let's head to `www.digitalocean.com` to register.

Note   If you are new to DigitalOcean, you can go to the following URL to get a $10 referral bonus: `https://bit.ly/in24hrs`.

Once you are registered and logged into the control panel, we can start creating the new cloud instance. DigitalOcean (DO) calls these instances *droplets*. For simplicity, we will refer to our cloud instance as an *instance* throughout the process.

If this is the first time that you are logging in and there are no instances that already exist, you may see a large blue button to initiate that creation of an instance. Alternatively, you can also click the green Create button in the top-right corner of the page and choose the Droplets option from the drop-down menu. Refer to the Figure 5-1 for more details. This takes you to the instance creation page. On this page, you specify various configuration options for our instance—select memory, space, and so forth. You have the option to select extensions or additional features. Although the most popular defaults are preselected, I highly recommend that you make a conscious choice for each specification.

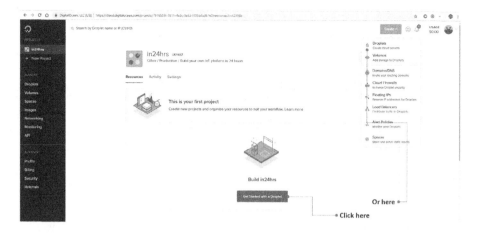

Figure 5-1. *Creating our cloud instance on DigitalOcean*

Choosing an Operating System Image

In this step, we choose the operating system for our IoT platform, and as
I explained earlier, we will select the Ubuntu distribution; however, there
are many other options to choose from. Refer to the Figure 5-2 for more
details. Under Container Distributions, we see containerized OS images. In
the One-Click Apps section, we see many preconfigured options to simply
get started. This option seems attractive, but it is worthwhile to spend time
choosing what we install.

For advanced usages, DigitalOcean offers a custom image option,
where we can upload a customized OS image. In many cases, this option
is handy when we want to replicate our IoT platform in multiple instances.
In this case, we can simply copy our existing image (with everything
installed) and upload it to the new instance. This makes things much faster
and more scalable.

Figure 5-2. *Select Ubuntu as an operating system image of choice*

Choosing the Size

Now that we have chosen the OS image, we need to specify the amount of RAM and disk space that we want. Since we need approximately 2 GB of RAM and about 50 GB of disk space for effective basic functioning, we will select the second choice from the standard table on the left-hand side as shown in the Figure 5-3. In the future, if we need to expand the instance specifications, we can easily do that with just a few clicks in about 5 minutes. Remember, we talked about building basic infrastructure in such a way that it can be scaled at any size we want; this is the way to do it. After selecting 2 GB RAM and 50 GB disk space, we have 2 TB of data transfer allowance. This is more than enough to begin with, and it will be enough for a long time—before our platform becomes very busy.

Choose a size

Standard Droplets

Balanced virtual machines with a healthy amount of memory tuned to host and scale applications like blogs, web applications, testing / staging environments, in-memory caching and databases.

MEMORY	vCPUs	SSD DISK	TRANSFER	PRICE
1 GB	1 vCPU	25 GB	1 TB	$5/mo $0.007/hr
2 GB	1 vCPU	50 GB	2 TB	$10/mo $0.015/hr
3 GB	1 vCPU	60 GB	3 TB	$15/mo $0.022/hr
2 GB	2 vCPUs	60 GB	3 TB	$15/mo $0.022/hr
1 GB	3 vCPUs	60 GB	3 TB	$15/mo $0.022/hr
4 GB	2 vCPUs	80 GB	4 TB	$20/mo $0.030/hr
8 GB	4 vCPUs	160 GB	5 TB	$40/mo $0.060/hr
16 GB	6 vCPUs	320 GB	6 TB	$80/mo $0.119/hr
32 GB	8 vCPUs	640 GB	7 TB	$160/mo $0.238/hr

CPU Optimized Droplets

Compute optimized virtual machines with dedicated hyper-threads from best in class Intel CPUs for CPU Intensive applications like CI/CD, video encoding, machine learning, ad serving, batch processing and active front-end web servers.

MEMORY	DEDICATED vCPUs	SSD DISK	TRANSFER	PRICE
4 GB	2 vCPUs	25 GB	4 TB	$40/mo $0.060/hr
8 GB	4 vCPUs	50 GB	5 TB	$80/mo $0.119/hr
16 GB	8 vCPUs	100 GB	6 TB	$160/mo $0.238/hr
32 GB	16 vCPUs	200 GB	7 TB	$320/mo $0.476/hr
64 GB	32 vCPUs	400 GB	9 TB	$640/mo $0.952/hr

Figure 5-3. *We will need approximately 2 GB of RAM and about 50 GB of disk space*

Note that CPU optimized instances are more suited for applications that heavily rely on CPU rather than RAM or disk and IO. Our IoT platform will eventually get to an enterprise-level system; however, at this stage, we are selecting only standard options. This also keeps the budget under control.

When we select a 64-bit operation system, as we did in the earlier step, 4 GB or more of RAM is advisable because we lose any benefits of the 64-bit system with a limited memory operation. From experience, it does not pose much of a problem, but it is easy to upscale, so let's go ahead with what we have selected so far.

Choosing a Datacenter Region

Now comes the step to select a datacenter region for our cloud instance as shown in the Figure 5-4. The only criterion that drives this selection is where our users are. Keeping servers near our end-users' geographic location improves performance by reducing server latency. If the user base is expected to be all over the world, the selection of a datacenter in the central part of the globe makes sense because it will keep latency almost the same for everyone. Although not an optimum choice, it is the best option when starting with just one small cloud instance. This is the reason that we select the London datacenter for our IoT platform since it is closer to the UTC.

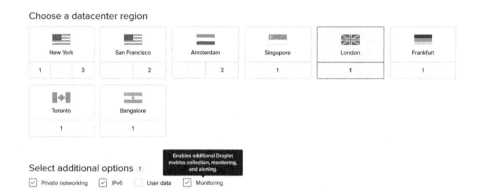

Figure 5-4. *Select the datacenter closer to UTC and activate additional options*

We will select additional options that allow us to easily use private networking and monitor our cloud instance. The private networking option enables an additional networking interface in the same datacenter for the instance. This way, if we have multiple cloud instances in the same datacenter, we can directly communicate with other instances without routing the traffic outside of the datacenter. IPv6 enables access to our cloud instance over IPv6. Remember that IPv6 is about future proofing, so there is no need to race to implement it, and you can reasonably ignore (and untick) this option.

Selecting the Monitoring option adds the DigitalOcean agent to your OS to collect extended metrics and create alert policies. This feature is free (at the time of writing of this book) and is helpful in monitoring and understanding traffic and other metrics related to our cloud instance.

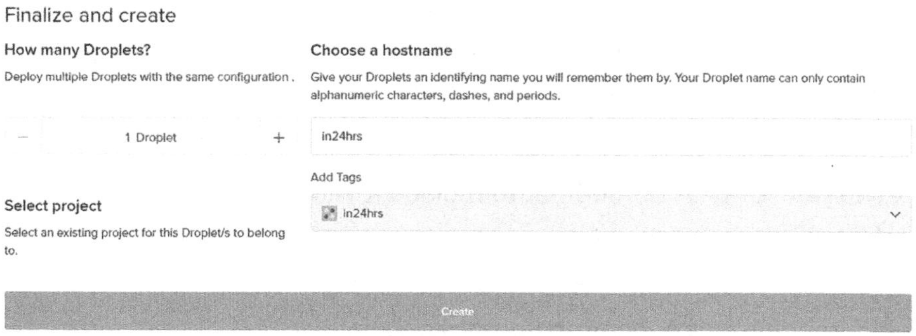

How many Droplets?

Deploy multiple Droplets with the same configuration .

— 1 Droplet +

Select project

Select an existing project for this Droplet/s to belong to.

Finalize and create

Choose a hostname

Give your Droplets an identifying name you will remember them by. Your Droplet name can only contain alphanumeric characters, dashes, and periods.

in24hrs

Add Tags

in24hrs

Create

Figure 5-5. *Give a meaningful hostname and then create*

Finalizing and Creating the Instance

Once we have chosen all the options, it is time to finalize the process and select a hostname for our cloud instance, as shown in the Figure 5-5. A hostname is used for control panel information and the server's hostname. Enter the hostname, keep the droplet (cloud instance) quantity at 1 because we are creating only one instance, and then click the Create button. This shows us a progress bar of our cloud instance creation.

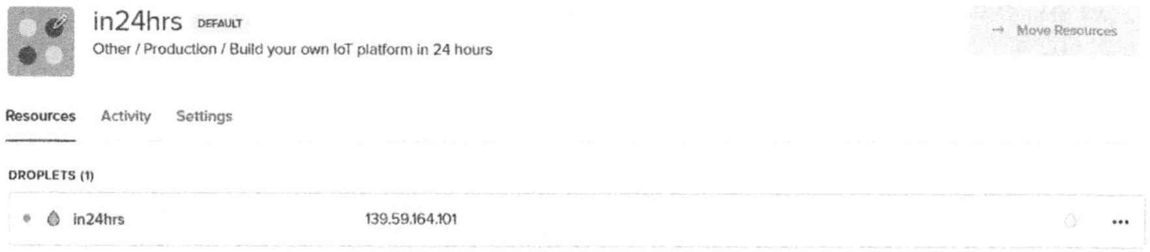

in24hrs DEFAULT
Other / Production / Build your own IoT platform in 24 hours

→ Move Resources

Resources   Activity   Settings

DROPLETS (1)

in24hrs   139.59.164.101   ...

Figure 5-6. *IP address for our cloud instance is displayed once process is complete*

When the process is complete, the IP address is assigned to our cloud instance and is visible on the control panel as shown in the Figure 5-6. Let's make a note of it because it is used all throughout the process. As seen in Figure 5-6, the IP address assigned to our cloud instance is 139.59.164.101.

49

Note   The assigned IP address is different in your case. Throughout this book, you should replace my IP address with your own. In some places, symbolic representation has been used, such as <INSTANCE_IP>. Remember to replace it with your actual IP address.

Connecting to Our Cloud Instance

Once the cloud instance is created, DigitalOcean will send an email that contains the IP address, the username, and the temporary password to log in the first time. Check for this email in your inbox; an email is sent to the same email address that was used during the registration of the account.

If you are using Linux or macOS, you can simply use the terminal to enter the ssh command to connect with our cloud instance. To connect, enter the following command:

```
# ssh root@<INSTANCE IP>
```

I have verified that on the latest Windows command line, the preceding command works as is. Depending on your IP address, the command will change. Note that the username in our case is *root*. Usually, the default Ubuntu OS distribution username is *root*. Since I use a Windows machine, I used PuTTY software for connectivity. The main dialog box of PuTTY program is shown in the Figure 5-7.

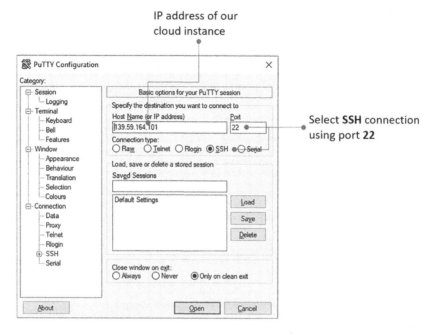

Figure 5-7. PuTTY connects with cloud instance on Windows OS

For the first connection, PuTTY shows a security alert dialog box that states that the server's host key is not cached in the registry. We should connect to this computer only if we know it will be secure. Since we are connecting to our own cloud instance, we hit the Yes button and move to the next step.

At the outset, the system prompts a password change. We begin by entering the default (temporary) password that we received via email. Once entered, we can change it to a new password of our choice.

Once we are logged in, the command prompt changes, and we see a welcome screen (see Figure 5-8). This marks the completion of the first step of initializing our cloud instance.

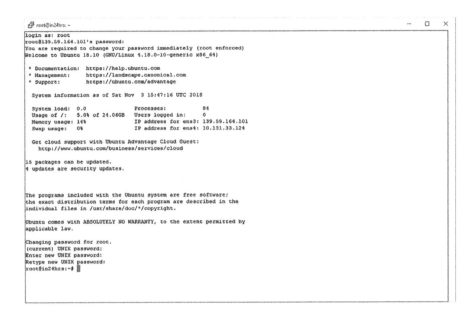

Figure 5-8. *The welcome screen for our cloud instance marks the completion of the first step*

Although not essential, we can also create a *floating IP* (a.k.a. *elastic IP*) for our cloud instance. It essentially provides an additional public static IP address that we can use to access our cloud instance without replacing its original IP.

Floating IPs are beneficial when creating high-availability cloud platforms. You can learn more about floating IPs at www.digitalocean. com/docs/networking/floating-ips/.

Installing Basic Software Stacks

Now that we have our cloud instance initialized and ready for further deployment, the installation of a LAMP stack is the next logical step. A LAMP stack is a set of open source software used to create websites and web applications. LAMP is an acronym that stands for

Linux-Apache-MySQL-PHP. It consists of the Linux operating system, an Apache HTTP Server, a MySQL relational database management system, and the PHP programming language.

Even before we start any kind of installation, let's get the base security up and running. We will start with enabling the firewall on our instance. Ubuntu servers use a firewall, and we can make sure that only connections to certain services are allowed by enabling it. We can set up a basic firewall very easily using this application.

Uncomplicated Firewall (UFW) is a program for managing a netfilter firewall designed to be easy to use. It uses a command-line interface consisting of a small number of simple commands and uses iptables for configuration. UFW is available by default in all Ubuntu installations after 8.04 LTS. (Uncomplicated Firewall, n.d.)

Applications can register their profiles with UFW after installation. UFW manages these applications by name, and we can see that the very service we have been using to connect with our cloud instance, the SSH utility, is already registered under OpenSSH. We can see which applications are registered by using UFW with the following command:

```
# ufw app list
```

Output
```
Available applications:
  OpenSSH
```

To make sure that the firewall allows SSH connections after enabling it, we will allow these connections, and then enable the firewall with the following two commands:

```
# ufw allow OpenSSH
# ufw enable
```

When we command enabling the firewall, the system prompts that it may disrupt the operation; press Y for *yes* in this case. Once the firewall is enabled, we can check the status with the status command.

```
# ufw status
```

Output
```
Status: active

To                          Action      From
--                          ------      ----
OpenSSH                     ALLOW       Anywhere
OpenSSH (v6)                ALLOW       Anywhere (v6)
```

Now except SSH. The firewall is blocking all the connections, and we have to configure additional applications each time we install them to accept inward traffic.

Installing Apache

Apache HTTP Server, colloquially called Apache, is a free and open source cross-platform web server software, released under the terms of Apache License 2.0. Apache is developed and maintained by an open community of developers under the auspices of the Apache Software Foundation. (Apache, n.d.)

It is among the most popular web servers in the world. It is well documented and is in wide use, and therefore a better choice. We can install Apache with the help of Ubuntu's package manager, called apt. Installation takes only two commands. During the process, it prompts for the extra disk it is going to use. Keep pressing Y and then Enter to continue until the installation is completed.

```
# apt update
# apt install apache2
```

Note   We have selected a single core instance for our purposes. However, as you move up to multicore processors, Apache may not provide the best performance. Eventually, options like NGINX should be evaluated.

Now that we have enabled the firewall, web server traffic will not be allowed, despite installing Apache. We have to add the Apache profile to the configuration. We allow web traffic with the following commands:

```
# ufw app list
```

Output
```
Available applications:
  Apache
  Apache Full
  Apache Secure
  OpenSSH
```

```
# sudo ufw app info "Apache Full"
```

Output
```
Profile: Apache Full
Title: Web Server (HTTP,HTTPS)
Description: Apache v2 is the next generation of the
omnipresent Apache web
server.
```

```
Ports:
  80,443/tcp
```

```
# sudo ufw allow in "Apache Full"
```

Output
```
Rule added
Rule added (v6)
```

In the preceding commands, the first command displays all the apps that have an application profile under UFW. Since we added Apache, it is shown in the command output. In the second command, we are checking that the Apache Full configuration allows web traffic at the HTTP (port 80) and HTTPS (port 443) ports. And with the third command, the profile is added to the UFW program.

At this stage, if we open our web browser and navigate to our cloud instance IP, we see the default Apache webpage (see Figure 5-9). It shows that Apache is now installed and working as expected.

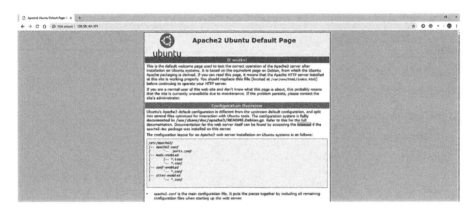

Figure 5-9. *Default Apache webpage*

Installing MySQL

With our web server installed and up and running, it is time to install the database management system. Since we have chosen MySQL, it will be a straightforward task with only a few commands, as follows:

```
# apt install mysql-server
```

When the preceding command is executed, the system prompts for the extra disk it is going to use. We keep pressing Y and then Enter to continue until the installation is completed. Apparently, MySQL comes with a default configuration installed, and it is a good idea to secure our installation right now. After the MySQL installation, there is a preinstalled script that helps us secure our database system. To start the process, execute the following command:

```
# mysql_secure_installation
```

This asks if we want to configure the validate password plugin. We will select Y for *yes* and continue providing additional passwords as prompted. When we provide a new password, the script shows the password strength for the root password we entered, and we have an opportunity to change it if we want to. We will skip this step and enter N for *no* at this stage.

For the rest of the questions, we keep pressing the Y and Enter keys at each prompt from the script. This essentially removes some default anonymous users and the test database. It also disables remote root logins and loads these new rules so that MySQL immediately enforces the changes that we just made.

For Ubuntu systems running the latest MySQL versions, the root user is authenticated using the auth_socket plugin by default instead of with a password. In many cases, it complicates the access, especially when we want other applications and external programs to connect with MySQL. We need to change it, and we can do this with the following commands, starting with opening the MySQL prompt on the command line.

```
# mysql
```

Output

```
Welcome to the MySQL monitor.  Commands end with ; or \g.
Your MySQL connection id is 7
Server version: 5.7.24-0ubuntu0.18.10.1 (Ubuntu)

Copyright (c) 2000, 2018, Oracle and/or its affiliates. All
rights reserved.
```

Oracle is a registered trademark of Oracle Corporation and/or its affiliates. Other names may be trademarks of their respective owners.

Type 'help;' or '\h' for help. Type '\c' to clear the current input statement.

mysql> SELECT user,authentication_string,plugin,host FROM mysql. user WHERE user="root";

Output

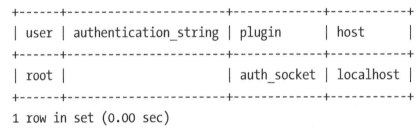

1 row in set (0.00 sec)

The second command lists the authentication method for the root user. And as we can see that the method is not what we want (i.e., password), we change it with an another command. We need a strong password handy while we issue the very first command.

mysql> ALTER USER 'root'@'localhost' IDENTIFIED WITH mysql_ native_password BY **'your-password'**;

Output
Query OK, 0 rows affected (0.00 sec)

mysql> FLUSH PRIVILEGES;

Output
Query OK, 0 rows affected (0.00 sec)

mysql> SELECT user,authentication_string,plugin,host FROM mysql.user WHERE user="root";

Output

```
+------+----------------------+---------------------+-----------+
| user | authentication_string | plugin             | host      |
+------+----------------------+---------------------+-----------+
| root | *A0AF1999141933B3B4C7
          AE72544AB01849669F98 | mysql_native_password| localhost |
+------+----------------------+ --------------------+-----------+
1 row in set (0.00 sec)
```

mysql> exit

Output

Bye

The first command provides a strong password of your choice. The second command reloads the table, and the new changes go into effect immediately. With the next command, we double-check the status of the authentication method for the root user, and as we can see in the output, it has changed as needed. With that, we can now exit the MySQL prompt with the exit command.

At this point, MySQL is installed, and we can install the final key component of LAMP stack—PHP.

Installing PHP

PHP stands for Hypertext Preprocessor, which is an open source, server-side scripting language for the development of web applications and services.

We will use Ubuntu's apt package manager to install PHP.

```
# apt install php libapache2-mod-php php-mysql
```

As you can see, in addition to the PHP package, we are also installing a few more packages. This will enable us to run PHP code on the Apache web server and communicate with the MySQL database easily. When the preceding command is executed, the system prompts for the extra disk that it is going to use. We keep pressing Y and then Enter to continue until the installation is completed.

By default, an Apache web server serves HTML files as a preference, and then looks for CGI and Perl files if the HTML file is not available. If the CGI or Perl file is not found, then it checks for a PHP file. However, since we wish to use PHP for our server-side programs in all cases, we need to change this behavior. We change the Apache directory configuration with the following commands:

```
# nano /etc/apache2/mods-enabled/dir.conf
```

This opens the configuration file in the default Ubuntu editor, called *nano*. This file has default file names listed in order, as shown next.

```
<IfModule mod_dir.c>
    DirectoryIndex index.html index.cgi index.pl index.php
    index.xhtml index.htm
</IfModule>
```

First, we change the order of the file names, starting with index.php followed by the index.html, and then the rest.

```
<IfModule mod_dir.c>
    DirectoryIndex index.php index.html index.htm index.cgi
    index.pl index.xhtml
</IfModule>
```

Once the changes are done, the file can be saved by pressing Ctrl+X and then typing **Y**, followed by pressing Enter. This exits us from the editor.

We restart the Apache web server to make these changes effective by using the following command:

```
# systemctl restart apache2
```

This silently restarts Apache web server and reloads the configurations with the new changes. However, we still need to validate that these changes are effective. To do so, we create a test PHP program file and verify it within the browser by navigating to the IP address of our cloud instance. To create a new test program, we open a new file with this command and add a few basic lines in the file.

```
# nano /var/www/html/test.php
```

Add these contents to the file
```
<?php
    echo("Hi...PHP is working !");
?>
```

Once finished, we save and close with the Ctrl+X combination followed by typing **Y** and then pressing Enter. Now when we navigate to http://<INSTANCE_IP>/test.php, we should see the message as shown in the Figure 5-10.

Figure 5-10. *Working PHP page in browser*

At this stage, our LAMP stack is fully functional, but before we move on to doing something useful with it, we need to strengthen the security. We also need to enable easy and efficient access to MySQL, preferably in a web browser environment, which can be done with the help of the phpMyAdmin program.

Securing the Instance and Software

Since we need an easy and efficient way to access MySQL functionality from the browser and at the same time maintain secure access, phpMyAdmin seems to be a better choice. phpMyAdmin is a free and open source administration tool for MySQL. As a portable web application written primarily in PHP, it has become one of the most popular MySQL administration tools. (phpMyAdmin, n.d.)

To begin the installation, we will first update the package index of our cloud instance. This is followed by the installation of base files for phpMyAdmin with the following two commands:

```
# apt update
```

```
# apt install phpmyadmin php-mbstring php-gettext
```

Note   While php-mbstring (multibyte string manipulation) and php-gettext (text handling) are not security-related packages, they are necessary for phpMyAdmin's functioning, and therefore required to be installed.

At this stage of the installation process, the system asks a few questions. On the first screen, we will select apache2 as the server; we use the spacebar to mark our selection while we move our choices using arrow keys. Once selected, the installation continues and then asks the next question with another prompt —"configure database for phpmyadmin with dbconfig-common". Select Yes.

Finally, it asks you to choose and confirm your MySQL application password for phpMyAdmin. After you input that, the installation is complete. At this stage, the installation has added the phpMyAdmin Apache configuration file to the /etc/apache2/conf-enabled/ directory, where it is read automatically. The only thing we now need to do is explicitly enable the *mbstring PHP extension*, which we can do by entering the following:

```
# phpenmod mbstring
# systemctl restart apache2
```

Now we can access the MySQL database with phpMyAdmin by navigating to http://<INSTANCE_IP>/phpmyadmin. It asks for credentials, which we just created. Upon providing the correct credentials, we are able to access our MySQL database in the browser, as shown in Figure 5-11.

Figure 5-11. *phpMyAdmin login screen and main interface in web browser*

Let's secure our phpMyAdmin instance. As we navigate to the phpMyAdmin page in the browser, we notice that the application asks for credentials. However, if the page is not accessed over SSL, our credentials could very well be intercepted. Moreover, the phpMyAdmin tool is so widely used that it is often a target of attack. However, we can add an extra layer of security by placing another credential gateway in front of the application. That means the user is unable to navigate to the login page without entering first-level credentials.

We can add this extra layer of security with the help of a commonly used method in Apache web servers (i.e., using .htaccess), authentication, and authorization functionality.

In the first step, we enable the use of `.htaccess` file overrides by editing the Apache configuration file for phpMyAdmin. This file is available in the configuration directory.

```
# nano /etc/apache2/conf-available/phpmyadmin.conf
```

Modify contents of the file as follows

```
Alias /phpmyadmin /usr/share/phpmyadmin

<Directory /usr/share/phpmyadmin>
    Options SymLinksIfOwnerMatch
    DirectoryIndex index.php
    AllowOverride All

    .....
    .....
```

Note that in the preceding file extract, we have added a directive as `AllowOverride All` within the `<Directory /usr/share/phpmyadmin>` section. This enables the use of the `.htaccess` file for authentication and authorization. Now we will create this required `.htaccess` file with four lines that allow authentication.

```
# nano /usr/share/phpmyadmin/.htaccess
```

Add following contents to the file
```
AuthType Basic
AuthName "Restricted Files"
AuthUserFile /etc/phpmyadmin/.htpasswd
Require valid-user
```

By adding the preceding contents, we are enabling a basic type of authentication that is done with the help of a password file. The second line in the file sets the message for the authentication dialog box. As a general guideline and best practice, let's keep it generic and simply state

"Restricted Files" so that the message does not give away too much information about what is behind the restriction.

The third line states the name of the password file and its location. Ideally, it should be outside of the directory being protected. And the final line asserts the authorization function, which stops unauthorized users from entering the directory and accessing the phpMyAdmin application. We will save and close with the Ctrl+X combination, followed by Y, and then Enter.

The next step is to create this password file and create the first user with a password. This is accomplished with the help of the htpasswd utility and the following commands:

```
# htpasswd -c /etc/phpmyadmin/.htpasswd username
```

```
# htpasswd /etc/phpmyadmin/.htpasswd additional_username
```

The first command creates the new file, named .htpasswd, and then adds a new user to it. Once we execute this command, the system prompts for a password and confirms it for this user. The passwords are stored in the hashed format in the file.

Notice that the second command is without the -c option, so it does not create a new file; instead, it uses an existing file (created by the first command) and adds another user as needed. We can add as many users as we want.

Now if we navigate to http://<INSTANCE_IP>/phpmyadmin, the browser first asks for Apache authentication before presenting the phpMyAdmin login page, as shown in Figure 5-12. Once we input the correct credentials, we are presented with the usual phpMyAdmin login page.

Figure 5-12. *Additional security for phpMyAdmin*

At this stage, phpMyAdmin is fully configured and ready for use. Using this interface makes it easy for us to create databases and tables, and to perform various database operations. This comes in handy as we progress to create time-series data storage and add various other data tables to use in the platform.

It's Easier with a Domain Name

While it is easy (for now) to access our cloud instance with its IP address, it will be even easier to use it with a proper fully qualified domain name (FQDN). It will also enable us to add transport layer security with TLS/SSL.

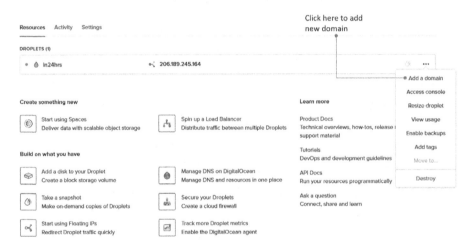

Figure 5-13. Adding a new domain on our cloud instance

Apparently, Let's Encrypt makes it a policy to not issue SSL certificates for IP addresses. We are unable to use the certificate by continuing with the IP address. Technically, we can install the certificate, but it is useless. Moreover, many browsers do not honor SSL over a bare IP address. So, it is a good idea to get a domain name for our IoT platform now. There are various options to get the required domain name. A simple search in Google shows the best options for you.

The first step is to get the desired domain from a domain registrar, and then head to the DigitalOcean control panel to make the required changes to the cloud instance DNS records. Instead of using a generic reference to the example.com domain, I used my own domain name, in24hrs.xyz, for ongoing references in this book.

Once a desired domain name is available, click Add Domain on the control panel, as shown in Figures 5-13 and 5-14 respectively.

Figure 5-14. *Provide domain name and click Add Domain*

In the next step, we update our nameservers with a domain registrar. This process usually differs by registrar, and each domain registrar has a step-by-step tutorial to explain how to change nameservers on their control panels. Note that DigitalOcean has the following three nameservers, which need to be updated in the domain registry:

ns1.digitalocean.com
ns2.digitalocean.com
ns3.digitalocean.com

After our domain name is configured and the relevant records have been updated on the control panel, we set up SSL certificates for our domain name. SSL certificates are available with various providers and the cost of those certificates could range from a few hundred dollars to thousands of dollars. However, there are many credible authorities that provide SSL certificates for free without compromising security; we will use one of those. If you already have an SSL certificate purchased from another authority, you can upload it on the cloud instance, and then go directly to the Apache configuration update step.

Note   Remember to use your chosen domain name when executing these steps and commands.

Note that before we begin the next steps, you need to set up the following two DNS records on your server control panel, which is also shown in Figure 5-15.

A record with **in24hrs.xyz** pointing to your server's **public IP** address.

A record with **www.in24hrs.xyz** pointing to your server's **public IP** address.

Figure 5-15. *Change A records in control panel*

Usually, nameserver and record changes take about an hour to reflect completely across the Web. After an hour, if we navigate to www.in24hrs.xyz in the browser, it should take us to the default Apache webpage on our cloud instance, as shown in Figure 5-9.

Add Virtual Hosts to Our Web Server

We need to have virtual hosts set up for Apache to use and configure our domain name effectively. The first step is to create a separate directory for our newly added domain. This is followed by assigning the ownership of the directory with the $USER environmental variable.

```
# mkdir -p /var/www/in24hrs.xyz/html
```

```
# chown -R $USER:$USER /var/www/in24hrs.xyz/html
```

Let's make sure that permissions have been set up correctly.

```
# chmod -R 755 /var/www/in24hrs.xyz
```

Now we will create a simple webpage to be displayed when we navigate to our domain name in the browser. We will create a PHP file since we already gave it preference in an earlier setup.

```
# nano /var/www/in24hrs.xyz/html/index.php
```

Add following contents to the file
```
<?php
    echo("Hi...this is our webpage with domain name !");
?>
```

For the Apache web server to serve this content, we need to create a virtual host file with the correct directives, and enable that configuration subsequently. We will also turn off the web server's default configuration and keep a separate copy of it for future reference and as a fallback option.

```
# nano /etc/apache2/sites-available/in24hrs.xyz.conf
```

Add following contents to the file
```
<VirtualHost *:80>
    ServerAdmin admin@in24hrs.xyz

    ServerName in24hrs.xyz
    ServerAlias www.in24hrs.xyz

    DocumentRoot /var/www/in24hrs.xyz/html

    ErrorLog ${APACHE_LOG_DIR}/error.log
    CustomLog ${APACHE_LOG_DIR}/access.log combined
</VirtualHost>
```

```
# a2ensite in24hrs.xyz.conf
```

Output
```
Enabling site in24hrs.xyz.
To activate the new configuration, you need to run:
  systemctl reload apache2
```

We will now disable the default configuration, and then run a configuration test to check for any errors that we might have made during the process. If you get an error, check for any typos and missing characters in the virtual host file.

```
# a2dissite 000-default.conf
```

Output
```
Site 000-default disabled.
To activate the new configuration, you need to run:
  systemctl reload apache2
```

```
# apache2ctl configtest
```

Output

```
Syntax OK

# systemctl restart apache2
```

With the last command, the Apache web server restarts and reloads the new configuration that we created earlier. At this stage, if we navigate to www.in24hrs.xyz, we should see the message Hi...this is our webpage with domain name! in our web browser, as shown in Figure 5-16.

Figure 5-16. *We are now able to access our cloud instance with a domain name*

Installing SSL Certificates

In this process, we will use Let's Encrypt, which is a certificate authority (CA) that provides an easy and automated way to obtain, install, and maintain free TLS/SSL certificates. This process is simplified and automated with the help of a software client called Certbot. Certbot attempts to automate almost all the required steps and needs only minor manual effort.

We will install Certbot from an active Ubuntu software repository, which tends to be the most updated version, with the following command:

```
# add-apt-repository ppa:certbot/certbot
```

Press Enter to accept the prompt, and the installation will progress. Then we will install Certbot's Apache package with the apt package manager.

```
# apt install python-certbot-apache
```

71

Since we have enabled UFW for the firewall, and we already enabled HTTPS traffic through Apache Full configuration, we should be good with firewall settings at this stage. If this is not done already, you need to do it before proceeding.

We will now obtain an SSL certificate for our domain name with the following command:

```
# certbot --apache -d in24hrs.xyz -d www.in24hrs.xyz
```

This command runs Certbot with an Apache plugin. The -d parameter specifies the domain names for which we are requesting SSL certificates. Since we are running this command for the very first time, it may prompt for an email address. Agree to the terms of service and so forth. Afterward, the script proceeds with verbose output, as follows:

```
Performing the following challenges:
http-01 challenge for in24hrs.xyz
http-01 challenge for www.in24hrs.xyz
Enabled Apache rewrite module
Waiting for verification...
Cleaning up challenges
Created an SSL vhost at /etc/apache2/sites-available/in24hrs.
xyz-le-ssl.conf
Enabled Apache socache_shmcb module
Enabled Apache ssl module
Deploying Certificate to VirtualHost /etc/apache2/sites-
available/in24hrs.xyz-le-ssl.conf
Enabling available site: /etc/apache2/sites-available/in24hrs.
xyz-le-ssl.conf
Deploying Certificate to VirtualHost /etc/apache2/sites-
available/in24hrs.xyz-le-ssl.conf
```

Once the certificate is deployed on our cloud instance, it asks us whether we want to make the HTTPS changes mandatory; to this we select option 2, and the configuration is updated accordingly. Once the configuration is updated, Apache web server reloads the configuration and restarts.

```
Please choose whether or not to redirect HTTP traffic to HTTPS,
removing HTTP access.
- - - - - - - - - - - - - - - - - - - - - - - - - - - - - - - - - - -
1: No redirect - Make no further changes to the webserver
   configuration.
2: Redirect - Make all requests redirect to secure HTTPS access.
   Choose this for new sites, or if you're confident your site
   works on HTTPS. You can undo this change by editing your web
   server's configuration.
- - - - - - - - - - - - - - - - - - - - - - - - - - - - - - - - - - -
Select the appropriate number [1-2] then [enter] (press 'c' to
cancel): 2
Enabled Apache rewrite module
Redirecting vhost in /etc/apache2/sites-enabled/in24hrs.xyz.
conf to ssl vhost in /etc/apache2/sites-available/in24hrs.xyz-
le-ssl.conf
- - - - - - - - - - - - - - - - - - - - - - - - - - - - - - - - - - -
Congratulations! You have successfully enabled
https://in24hrs.xyz and
https://www.in24hrs.xyz
```

The preceding settings also ensure that HTTP traffic is redirected to HTTPS. To check if everything is working as expected, navigate to www.in24hrs.xyz in your browser, you should see the output as shown in Figure 5-17. Our certificates are downloaded, installed, and loaded automatically, and they will be automatically renewed on a quarterly basis—thanks to Certbot automation.

Figure 5-17. *HTTPS enabled on domain name*

When navigating to `www.in24hrs.xyz`, you will notice that the browser is now showing a lock icon next to the website name (usually, it is green in Firefox and gray in Chrome).

We can check our cloud instance SSL certificates at `www.ssllabs.com/ssltest/analyze.html?d=www.in24hrs.xyz`, here the website will perform some tests and tell us the level of security through SSL report on the given website being tested as shown in Figure 5-18.

Figure 5-18. *SSL certificates are valid and has an A*

At this stage, our general web interface is ready and available to use over SSL. We are also able to use phpMyAdmin over SSL, which will strengthen database security further.

Installing Node.js and Node-RED

Node.js is a JavaScript platform for general-purpose programming that allows users to build network applications quickly. By leveraging JavaScript on both the front and back end, Node.js makes development more consistent and integrated. (DigitalOcean, n.d.)

We will use Ubuntu's apt package manager to update and install Node.js on our cloud instance with the following commands:

```
# apt update
```

```
# apt install nodejs
```

```
# apt install npm
```

In the preceding three commands, the first command refreshes the local package index, and the next command installs Node.js on our instance. We are also installing the node package manager, NPM, which helps us update and add node packages to our instance as needed.

For each of the installations, we are prompted with the amount of disk space being used; we are selecting Y for *yes* in both cases.

Upon successful installation, we can check the installed version of each application with the following commands:

```
# nodejs -v
```

Output
```
V8.11.4
```

```
# npm -v
```

Output
```
5.8.0
```

Once we have installed the node package manager, it is easier to install Node-RED with the same package manager. We will install Node-RED as a global module so that it will add the node-red command to our cloud's system path.

```
npm install -g --unsafe-perm node-red
```

The preceding command installs Node-RED and its dependencies at once. Ideally, if we navigate with our browser, we are able to use Node-RED directly. However, recall that we enabled the firewall with UFW and closed off all the inbound traffic unless explicitly approved. Due to this, we are unable to access Node-RED without enabling this traffic.

Additionally, since we have also mandated all the inbound traffic to be over HTTPS, we need to modify the Node-RED configuration to enable HTTPS. By default, Node-RED can run without SSL. Node-RED runs on default port 1880; therefore, we will enable traffic on that port first.

```
# ufw allow 1880/tcp
```

Output
```
Rule added
Rule added (v6)
```

At this stage, we can run Node-RED and check that the default interface is loading by navigating to our website by using our public IP address, http://<INSTANCE_IP>:1880 as shown in Figure 5-19. This is because we have not yet enabled SSL for Node-RED, and so we are unable to access it with our domain name directly. Run Node-RED now with the following command, and then navigate to the address mentioned earlier.

```
# node-red
```

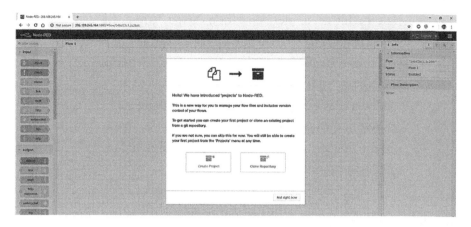

Figure 5-19. *Accessing Node-RED admin panel using public IP address*

Modifying Node-RED Settings

Let's modify the Node-RED configuration for better accessibility and functionality now. This primarily involves modifying the settings.js file that is available in the node-red root directory. We will do these changes using any standard editor available on our system (i.e., nano).

Note that at this stage, we are able to access the cloud instance using any compatible FTP program, such as FileZilla, using our normal root login credentials. FileZilla enables us to download a file from our cloud server, and then open, edit, and save it before uploading it back to the instance.

This can be done in three easy steps.

1. Connect the FileZilla FTP client to our cloud instance with a public IP address and login credentials.

2. Locate the file you want to edit. Then right-click the file that you want to edit. This opens the file with the default editor program installed on your computer. In most cases, it is Notepad, TextMate, or Notepad++.

3. Edit the file as needed, and then save it. When you save the file, FileZilla displays a window that alerts you about the file being changed and asks whether you wish to upload the file back to the server. If the file already exists, it also asks if you want to overwrite the existing file. After clicking the Yes option, a newly edited/created file is uploaded in the destination folder.

Caution   When using the edit feature in FileZilla, all the uploads are live. This means that when you upload the changed or new file, changes are in effect almost immediately on the cloud instance or website. I recommend that you download the copy of the original file while making any changes, and then consciously upload it when done. It is also a good practice to maintain an exact replica of important folders on our cloud server on your local machine, so that you can easily navigate to required files as needed.

Now let's get back to editing the settings file. Starting at the beginning of the file, we uncomment the fs module declaration and make it available, as follows:

```
// The `https` setting requires the `fs` module. Uncomment the
   following
// to make it available:
var fs = require("fs");
```

Enabling the fs module is required because we want to enable HTTPS on our Node-RED instance. At line 93 in the settings file, we uncomment the admin root path. This enables us to access the Node-RED editor at different endpoints than the root URL. While it is not mandatory to do this, it is useful because we can then utilize the root URL for any other purpose, such as hosting different webpages and information pages, and so forth.

```
// The following property can be used to specify a different
   root path.
// If set to false, this is disabled.
httpAdminRoot: '/admin',
```

Now let's modify a block between lines 138 and 147. This block enables HTTPS for Node-RED, and we must provide a private key and a certificate file name to enable it. We must provide the full file path, which we can obtain in one of two ways. We can refer to the SSL installation output, on which the end of the process script shows where files are stored, or alternatively, the path can be copied from the Apache configuration file that is available at /etc/apache2/sites-available/in24hrs.xyz.conf.

```
// The following property can be used to enable HTTPS
// See http://nodejs.org/api/https.html#https_https_createserver_
   options_requestlistener
// for details on its contents.
// See the comment at the top of this file on how to load the
   `fs` module used by
// this setting.
https: {
    key: fs.readFileSync("/etc/letsencrypt/live/in24hrs.xyz/
    privkey.pem"),
    cert: fs.readFileSync("/etc/letsencrypt/live/in24hrs.xyz/
    cert.pem")
},
```

Since we are building our own IoT platform, which will eventually be used on various systems and devices, cross-origin resource sharing is required. It is a good idea to enable it right now in the settings file by uncommenting the relevant block between lines 162 and 165, as follows.

```
// The following property can be used to configure cross-origin
   resource sharing in the HTTP nodes.
// See https://github.com/troygoode/node-cors#configuration-
   options for details on its contents. The following is a
   basic permissive set of options:
httpNodeCors: {
    origin: "*",
    methods: "GET,PUT,POST,DELETE"
},
```

A completely modified `settings.js` file can be downloaded from the GitHub repository.

Securing our Node-RED Editor

With the new file saved on the disk, now we can run our Node-RED instance using our domain name over HTTPS instead of a public IP. Check that the editor interface is loading by navigating to our website at www. in24hrs.xyz:1880/admin.

You can see the editor directly without any authentication or login page, and now we will fix that by enabling security for Node-RED. To begin, we have to install some admin tools for Node-RED with the following commands:

```
# npm install -g node-red-admin
```

Some errors or warnings may appear at this stage, but they can be ignored for now. In the next step, we create a user/password credential pair for the Node-RED editor login with the following command:

```
# node-red-admin hash-pw
```

The tool prompts for the password that we wish to use, and then prints the hash, which can be copied and pasted into the settings.js file in the next step.

Let's open the settings file and have a look at the code block near line 122. We will uncomment that code block and add a username in plain text; the password is *hash,* which we copied in the previous step. I have created two users, so there are two different hashes for each of them. For one user, admin, we are allowing full access; for a guest user, it is read-only access.

```
// Securing Node-RED
// -----------------
// To password protect the Node-RED editor and admin API, the
    following property can be used. See http://nodered.org/docs/
    security.html for details.
adminAuth: {
    type: "credentials",
    users: [
    {
            username: "admin",
            password: "$2a$08$NeGbPtKiHU4JCC.IyqGz3tG2PeV.
                    W8As9NEa62F9HX.qGz3tEA79mm",
            permissions: "*"
    },
    {
            username: "guest",
            password: "$2a$08$Fg/yRxn8As9NEa6435SvdNeGbPtKiOe/
                    IyqGz3tG2PeV.A.UvRaTIXe",
            permissions: "read"
    }
    ]
},
```

Once this change has completed and the settings file is uploaded, we have to restart the program with the node-red command, and then navigate to www.in24hrs.xyz:1880/admin. This time, we see a login page asking for credentials, as shown in Figure 5-20.

When we start Node-RED, it runs on the command line with verbose output, which essentially means that we cannot do anything else while it is running. We can run Node-RED as a service in the background with a simple command, as follows:

```
# node-red > node-red.log &
```

With this command, the Node-RED output log is redirected to the node-red.log file, and & at the end tells Ubuntu to run the program as *daemon* (i.e., in the background).

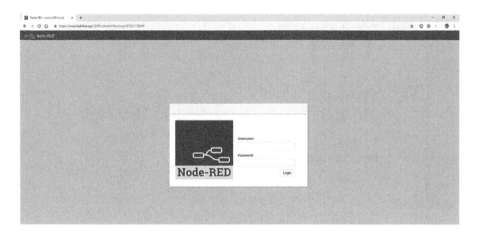

Figure 5-20. *Secured Node-RED editor login*

Summary

We now have a fully operational cloud instance that has almost all the essentials that we need to build our own IoT platform. The next step is to start building the plumbing of the platform by adding the required blocks of services.

As explained in previous chapters, the message broker is one of the critical components, and therefore it is important that we understand its functionality. I elaborate on the message broker in the next chapter.

CHAPTER 6

The Message Broker

In Chapter 4, we chose MQTT as our messaging protocol. We are going to use the Mosquitto program as a broker for this purpose. In this chapter, we elaborate more on MQTT and cover the following:

- How a pub/sub paradigm works

- The various features and functionalities of MQTT

- WebSocket

- When to utilize the message broker

- How to install and secure MQTT on our cloud instance

Let's dive into MQTT and how the message broker block will play an important role in our IoT platform.

What Is MQTT?

MQTT is a client-server publish/subscribe messaging transport protocol. It is lightweight, open, simple, and designed to be easy to implement. These characteristics make it ideal for use in many situations, including constrained environments such as for communication in machine-to-machine (M2M) and Internet of Things (IoT) contexts, where a small code footprint is required and/or network bandwidth is at a premium. (OASIS Standard - MQTT Version 3.1.1, 2015)

© Anand Tamboli 2019
A. Tamboli, *Build Your Own IoT Platform*, https://doi.org/10.1007/978-1-4842-4498-2_6

MQTT is a very lightweight and binary type protocol, and due to minimal packet overheads, it is easy to implement on constrained devices. This makes it ideal for IoT devices (a.k.a. things).

Publish and Subscribe Paradigm

As with HTTP interaction using client-server architecture, MQTT uses pub/sub architecture. As an inherent requirement, it needs to have a message broker in between. This essentially decouples one publisher (or sending client) from the subscriber (or receiving client). Moreover, this also means that we can have more than one subscriber to the same published message.

Let's understand how the publish and subscribe paradigm works with the help of a simple arrangement, as depicted in Figure 6-1. There are five clients (a.k.a. things) connected to the message broker via an Internet connection. Each client plays a different role.

- Clients A and B are sensor devices transmitting temperature and humidity, respectively.

- Client C is a connected fan.

- Client D is a laptop.

- Client E is a mobile application.

As clients C, D, and E need to act on the information published by A and B, they are subscribers to the temperature and humidity information (topic). Sensor clients A and B regularly transmit temperature and humidity data (payload) on respective channels (topics). The message broker is responsible for keeping track of who is connected and which topics they are subscribed to.

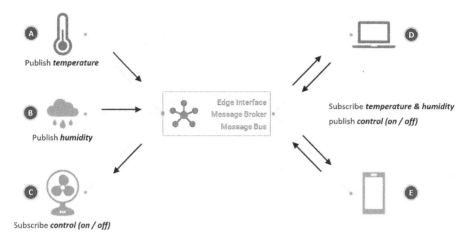

Figure 6-1. *Publish and subscribe paradigm*

Whenever clients A and B publish the information, clients C, D, and E receive it.

The advantage of a pub/sub paradigm is that even if one of the clients is down, it does not break the system. The broker helps decouple clients on various levels, so that they cannot remain connected to the broker at the same time, and they do not need to be time synchronized.

The pub/sub mechanism also allows us to enable better message routing and event-based actions. This is important for our IoT platform because it improves overall architecture and keeps it clean. Scalability of architecture is another aspect of why we are using MQTT and pub/sub on the platform.

As an independent client, each node in the system can contribute its information to a larger ecosystem. That means that we can enable fan C to act based on the readings of clients A and B, as well as the readings from other temperature sensors outside the diagram, (e.g., a weather forecasting or environmental monitoring system).

Other Features of a Message Broker and MQTT

In general, the term *client* refers to everything that is connected to or communicating through the MQTT message broker. Thus, the client can be the publisher of the information, the subscriber of the information, or both. Since MQTT is a TCP/IP-based protocol, any device that can speak TCP/IP should be able to establish an MQTT connection and become a client. In practice, there might be different constraints that could prevent this from happening; however, the protocol is designed to work with constrained devices.

We can have sensors and control system devices acting as clients; similarly, we can have other computers, mobile phones, or web applications acting as clients and/or sensors. All of them put together in a meaningful way eventually makes a working and useful solution.

A *broker*, on the other hand, is a coordinator or an orchestrator of this communication. It is a broker's job to receive all the messages from all the clients, filter them, look up which client is subscribed to what topic, and then redistribute the messages to those clients. The broker is also responsible for maintaining various connection parameters, such as client session details, credentials, the database of stored (a.k.a. retained) messages, and a few other things.

As the broker performs such an important and pivotal role in the pub/sub communication system, it is expected to be highly available; fault tolerant; easy to deploy, monitor, and maintain; and easy to integrate with several other aspects of the full solution. Our chosen broker, Mosquitto, passes all of these criteria.

Quality of Service

There is an interesting concept with the pub/sub mechanism known as QoS, or *quality of service*. Quality of service is one of the critical and highly useful features of MQTT communication. Despite being lightweight and non-verbose in nature, the MQTT protocol enables clients to maintain a consistent connection with a broker over a long period of time and ensures that all the messages that are published or subscribed are delivered with some level of guarantee. This guarantee is maintained in the form of the MQTT message "QoS".

QoS is an agreement between the sender and the receiver of a message. It must be noted that as far as the pub/sub mechanism is concerned, there are at least two senders and two receivers. This is because each message passes through the broker. Thus, for any sent message, the broker is the first receiver and then there is the subsequent receiver(s) and vice versa. Therefore, QoS in an MQTT context works at these two levels.

There are three QoS levels supported by MQTT.

- *QoS 0.* At most once (a.k.a. "fire and forget") means that the message can be lost

- *QoS 1.* At least once (i.e., there could be duplicates)

- *QoS 2.* Exactly once

There are times when the subscriber QoS level is different from the publisher's QoS level. That is, a publisher sends a message with the intention of sending it precisely once (QoS 2); however, if a subscriber is not interested in that level of certainty, it can subscribe the message at QoS 0. Therefore, when the broker tries to deliver this message to a subscriber, the QoS is downgraded as requested by the subscriber. Contrarily, if a subscriber has requested a higher service level than the publisher, it is upgraded to the subscriber's request too.

The QoS mechanism helps select appropriate service levels of communication to match the operational environment of the clients. If a client is in a highly unreliable communication environment connection over 3G in a moving vehicle, for example, then those clients can select a higher QoS to ensure that they receive the communication. Clients working in a reliable communication zone, such as in a home with Wi-Fi connectivity, can choose a lower QoS level because the connectivity is expected to be reliable.

In general, QoS 0 should be selected when the connectivity is reliable, and the loss of a message or messages would not cause any issues. QoS 1 is often the optimum choice because messages are received at least once, and duplicate messages could be handled at an application layer, if received. If each message is critical and must not be skipped or missed, QoS 2 is highly recommended. Note that we can always implement application-level logic to maintain and upgrade the reliability of the communication without the help of a protocol; having protocol support at a protocol layer is an added advantage, though.

Keep Alive Period

The MQTT protocol is fully duplex and has live communication, which means that both sides of the communication must be connected and live. In a pub/sub mechanism, the broker and client should be connected and are live when communicating. If the link breaks for any reason (non-reliable network, etc.), then each of the parties should know that this happened and then act accordingly.

The fundamental TCP protocol on which MQTT is based does not necessarily work that way in practice (in theory, it must), which means that when there is a broken connection, one of the two parties may not know that the connection is broken. This situation is called a *half-open connection*. To deal with such a scenario, *keep alive* was introduced.

The *keep alive period* is the maximum time interval that is permitted to elapse between the point at which the client finishes transmitting one control packet and the point that it starts sending the next. It is the responsibility of the client to ensure that the interval between control packets being sent does not exceed the keep alive value. In the absence of sending any other control packets, the client must send a PINGREQ packet. (OASIS Standard - MQTT Version 3.1.1, 2015)

In short, if there is some data flow between the client and the broker that occurs in less time than the period specified by the keep alive interval, the connection will remain active and verifiably full. If there is no data flow, then the client sends a two-byte transmission (in the form of a PINGREQ packet) to let the broker know. If the client does not send a keep alive packet or any data within that interval, the broker closes the connection and publishes a last-will message, as set by the client during the connection.

Although it may seem that a short keep alive interval is beneficial for data quality/currency/accuracy, it can backfire if too many non-trajectory messages are sent. This may happen as the broker, network, and other resources are applied toward the overhead, which may slow message handling.

Note   The maximum interval for keep alive is 18 hours, 12 minutes, and 15 seconds, which is 65,535 seconds. If you set the keep alive interval to 0, this mechanism is deactivated.

Last Will and Testament

As discussed, when a client does not send a keep alive packet or any data to the broker, the connection is closed, and the broker publishes a special message known as a *last will and testament* (LWT) to all the subscribers. This enables all other subscribers and applications to act in a meaningful way in the event of a client's ungraceful disconnection.

Note that "graceful disconnection" refers to the willful disconnection of any device or client from the message broker with a proper protocol handshake. If this does not happen (i.e., the disconnection is caused by an external factor, such as network blip), then the broker immediately releases an LWT message to all the subscribers.

Whenever a new connection is established by the client, one of the many parameters used for this connection is a *last-will-message*. Much like any other published message by the client, this is a client message, with the caveat that it is not published unless the client disconnects ungracefully. LWT is the best way to notify all the other subscribers about the disconnection and to let them act accordingly.

The Retained Message

A *retained message* is just like any other published message by the client. The *retained* flag is set to 1, or true, which instructs the broker to keep a copy of the message until it is erased or replaced. Whenever any subscriber subscribes to a topic or a pattern matching the retained message's topic, the message is immediately delivered.

It must be noted that there is only one retained message per topic, which presents an interesting way to keep every device and application updated with the current status of everything else. Figure 6-1 shows how we can establish such a mechanism.

In Figure 6-1, client A (a temperature sensor) connects to the broker the first time and while connected. It sets the LWT message as "offline" and the topic is "temp-sensor/status" with the retained flag set to true. It tells the broker to store this message until overwritten or deleted by the client, and to publish it only if the temperature sensor disconnects randomly. When a connection is established, the sensor immediately publishes another message as "online" on the same topic as "temp-sensor/status" and with the retained flag set to true.

Now any new client subscribing to temp-sensor/status will always receive "online" in response. However, if the temperature sensor is disconnected, the broker publishes its LWT message, and all the subscribers receive an offline message instantly. This keeps every other client updated with the temp-sensor's online status. Alternatively, if the sensor wants to disconnect, then it can first publish a message on the same topic as disconnected, indicating to all the clients that the sensor has willfully disconnected from the broker.

Retained messages with LWT are an effective way to establish a mechanism to always keep the status of every client updated.

To remove a retained message from the broker's storage, simply publish an empty message on the same topic. For example, if temp-sensor/status publishes an empty (0 byte) string with the retained flag set to true, the existing message value will be overwritten and not retained based on the new retention flag.

The Best Part: WebSocket

We have seen how and why MQTT is important from a communication perspective, on the Internet of Things in general, and especially for our own IoT platform. Therefore, it is naturally expected that we can use this functionality in browser-based apps that use the platform. WebSocket enables all MQTT features to the browser-based application, which then could be used in many interesting and useful working cases.

Browsers do not speak to TCP directly (yet), however, and therefore cannot speak to MQTT either. We need to leverage the existing capability of browsers to speak to the WebSocket protocol. WebSocket is a network protocol that provides bidirectional communication between a browser and the web server. This protocol was standardized in 2011, and almost all modern browsers provide built-in support for it. The good thing is that the WebSocket protocol is based on TCP, the same as MQTT, which is why it is easier.

Modern browsers and HTML5 introduced many new features that enable us to build websites that behave like desktop and mobile applications. Progressive web apps (PWAs) is a classic example. A browser is ubiquitously installed on almost every device, such as a desktop computer, laptop, notebook, or smartphone.

The consistency we can achieve by using a common protocol for all communication with heterogeneous devices and systems is the most tempting reason to use MQTT over WebSocket. Using MQTT with WebSocket also enables our applications to communicate over a live two-way channel. From live multiparty chats to live monitoring and control of systems, the opportunities are endless. We will enable and implement MQTT over WebSocket later in the book, once most of the platform is built and ready.

Are We Using the Best Message Broker Option?

There are several options for developing a message broker with full duplex functionalities and various supporting features. Some of these options are the use of a raw TCP socket, a raw UDP socket, AMQP, and CoAP. Most of these alternatives have more limitations and complications than benefits, especially when compared to MQTT. This is where MQTT becomes the most appropriate, efficient, and convenient choice, especially for building our own IoT platform.

Remember that all of these protocols can coexist, and we could deploy on the same cloud instance, if necessary. This means that in the future, if you decide to use AMQP as well as MQTT, it is possible to integrate some or all of them. More importantly, we can link these channels with additional plugin program(s) so that there is a seamless communication from an applications and devices perspective. It is out of the scope for this book but certainly possible.

When to Utilize a Message Broker and When Not To

Fundamentally, MQTT is an asynchronous protocol and thus enables duplex communication with a lightweight burden on systems. It allows systems to run on low bandwidth and low power. Contrarily, HTTP and similar protocols require relatively high bandwidth and power and are request-response in nature, which means that the client must always initiate communication.

In places where you want either party (server or client) to initiate communication, MQTT is the best choice. Moreover, if systems need to run on low data consumption, especially on batteries, for a long period, it is prudent to use MQTT. If the device needs to send or receive data frequently and at random, then MQTT also makes sense because it reduces a significant HTTP overhead.

If bandwidth and power is not a concern, then HTTP may be a better choice. Also, when data sending or receiving frequency is not high, which can block the resources sooner in the process.

In an application, where a live control or monitoring is required, MQTT is an obvious choice, because it provides duplex and two-way communication abilities with the least amount of overhead.

You must be mindful of the fact that the workload of an MQTT-based system can grow parabolically, which means that for each device added to the MQTT speaking network that has n devices in total, the load on the system becomes n squared $(n*n)$. Figure 6-2 explains this concept graphically.

For example, let's assume an extreme scenario where there are two clients in which each subscribes to all possible topics (*wildcard #*). When a client publishes a message, the broker needs to receive a message and another client needs to receive the message too. This means one message sent could result in two transmissions. The same goes for the other client, making it four messages in total for a two-client system. For a three-client system, this number becomes nine messages in total, (i.e., three messages per client). Simply having 100 devices connected means that the message broker should be capable of handling 10*10 (i.e., 100 messages, and so on).

This means that when the number of clients starts to grow, the load on the message broker and overall system (and platform) will grow almost exponentially; we need to keep this in mind as we scale our IoT platform in the later stages.

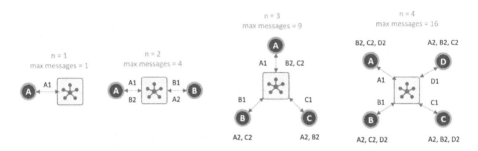

Figure 6-2. *MQTT-based platform load increases by n-square*

Installing a Message Broker

Now that we have discussed the fundamentals of a pub/sub mechanism and the way that a broker functions, let's install and configure the MQTT broker on our cloud instance. We will install the Mosquitto broker on our system. The Ubuntu repository has the latest version of Mosquitto available to install through **apt** package manager.

apt update

apt install mosquitto mosquitto-clients

The first command updates the package list, while the second command installs the Mosquitto broker and local client package. Once

installed, Mosquitto starts immediately, and we can check the same with
the following command:

```
# lsof -i :1883
```

Output
```
COMMAND     PID       USER  FD  TYPE  DEVICE   SIZE/OFF  NODE  NAME
mosquitto   352   mosquitto  3u  IPv4  1131147       0t0  TCP   local
                                                                host:1883
                                                                (LISTEN)
```

By default, Mosquitto listens on a standard MQTT port 1883, and we
can see in the output that the program is running and listening on that
port. At this stage, we can run a quick check to see if everything is working
as expected. To do that, we open another terminal window and log in for
a second time. Let's keep two windows open side by side to see what is
going on.

On one terminal, we subscribe to testTopic with the following
command:

```
# mosquitto_sub -h localhost -t testTopic
```

Here, -h specifies the hostname and -t specifies the subscription
topic. After sending the command, we do not see anything output because
the client that we just created is listening for new messages and nothing
has been sent yet.

On the other terminal, we publish a test message on testTopic as
follows:

```
# mosquitto_pub -h localhost -t testTopic -m "Hello world !"
```

The additional -m option is for specifying a message for the given
topic. Once the command is sent, you should see this message pop up on
another terminal that has subscribed to this testTopic. This confirms that
the Mosquitto broker is working fine on our cloud instance.

Now we can exit one of the terminals and stop the subscription command to continue with further setup. Press Ctrl+C to stop the subscription command. In the next step, we secure our Mosquitto broker with a username-password setup.

Securing a Message Broker

Mosquitto installation includes a utility to help generate a special password file called mosquitto_passwd. This places the results (i.e., username-password combination) in /etc/mosquitto/passwd in a hashed, unreadable format. To generate a password for the user named *anand*, use the following command:

```
# mosquitto_passwd -c /etc/mosquitto/passwd anand
```

```
# mosquitto_passwd /etc/mosquitto/passwd guest
```

Once sent, we are asked to input the password, which is stored in the password file subsequently. Option -c in the command tells the program to create a new password file, if it does not already exist. Use this option only the first time. The second command adds another user, named *guest*, and the respective password for that user.

For the changes to take effect, we need to add these details to the Mosquitto configuration, and then restart the Mosquitto broker. To do this, we first open the configuration file and add the relevant details to it. Then we restart the broker.

```
# nano /etc/mosquitto/conf.d/broker.conf
```

Add following lines to the file
```
allow_anonymous false
password_file /etc/mosquitto/passwd
```

```
# lsof -I :1883
```

Output

```
COMMAND      PID      USER    FD   TYPE    DEVICE   SIZE/OFF NODE  NAME
mosquitto    352   mosquitto  3u   IPv4   1131147       0t0  TCP   local
                                                                   host:
                                                                   1883
                                                                   (LISTEN)
```

```
# kill 352
```

In the first command, a new file opens, where we add two lines. The first line sets the configuration so that no anonymous client/user is allowed to connect with the broker. Only users listed in the mosquitto_passwd file can connect. The second line specifies the location of the password file so that the broker can authenticate each connection request. The broker uses the username-password combination from the file.

For the changes to be effective, we need to restart the broker; but this time, we also need to specify the configuration file that we just created. So first, we stop the service by killing the Mosquitto process that is already running. We do that in two steps: first, we find out the process ID (a.k.a. PID from the lsof command), and then send kill signal to that PID.

Next, we start the broker again with the configuration file, as follows:

```
# mosquitto -c /etc/mosquitto/conf.d/broker.conf -v &
```

In the command, -c specifies the configuration file to be loaded, -v specifies the verbose output, and & tells the system to keep running the broker in daemon mode (i.e., in the background without blocking the terminal).

Changes go into effect soon after our next command, which restarts the broker. Now if you try to publish any message as per the previous command, it will not work, and we will get an error: Connection Refused: not authorised. Error: The connection was refused.

In addition to listening on default port 1883, Mosquitto can use another port, 8883, for secure communications. This port adds TLS-based connectivity to the broker. We have secured our domain

99

(www.in24hrs.xyz) with SSL certificates. We can use the same certificate for securing Mosquitto. In addition to that, let's add a few more details to the configuration file by reopening the configuration file, broker.conf, and adding these details:

```
# nano /etc/mosquitto/conf.d/broker.conf
```

Add following lines to the file
```
# enable logging
log_type all
log_timestamp true
log_dest stdout
log_dest topic
sys_interval 15

# save the log every 15 mins
connection_messages true
autosave_interval 900
```

These lines tell the broker to log all the activity, which includes new connections, subscriptions, publishings, disconnects, errors, and warnings. This is useful from a debugging perspective, as well as for analyzing how the broker is working and what is going on while it functions. Note that comments in the conf file can be added with # at the beginning of the line.

We are also enabling connection messages for logging, so every new client connection request will be logged. This includes unauthorized and denied clients too. It is helpful to know if any unauthorized client(s) are trying to connect, or if authorized clients are unable to connect. It also logs the IP addresses of incoming connections. These details are saved in a log file every 900 seconds (15 minutes), as specified by the autosave interval.

```
# enable persistence in sessions
```

```
persistence true
persistence_file broker_log.txt
persistence_location /var/lib/mosquitto/
```

We are enabling persistence. The details of persisted sessions are stored in the broker_log.txt file. This file is saved in a directory, as specified in persistence_location.

```
# do not allow anonymous clients
allow_anonymous false
password_file /etc/mosquitto/passwd
```

We added two lines to our configuration file to stop all anonymous connections and provide a password file for authentication.

```
# secure open port for localhost only
listener 1883 localhost
```

```
# listen on secure connection with our SSL certificates
listener 8883
certfile /etc/letsencrypt/live/in24hrs.xyz/cert.pem
cafile /etc/letsencrypt/live/in24hrs.xyz/chain.pem
keyfile /etc/letsencrypt/live/in24hrs.xyz/privkey.pem
```

Here we have added two MQTT listeners in the configuration. The first listener is on port 1883, which is a standard, unencrypted MQTT port. We are setting up this port as localhost so that Mosquitto will bind it to the localhost, and it will not be externally accessible. This port can be used for any local applications for communicating over MQTT without any hassles.

The second listener is set up on port 8883, which is a standard, encrypted MQTT port, often referred as MQTTS (for MQTT Secure). The three lines after the declaration specify the locations of the certificate files. These locations were obtained when we installed SSL certificates for our domain in Chapter 5.

We save the configuration file and restart the broker by killing the old process.

```
# lsof -I :1883
```

Output

```
COMMAND     PID       USER  FD   TYPE   DEVICE SIZE/OFF  NODE  NAME
mosquitto   831  mosquitto  3u   IPv4  1131147      0t0   TCP  local
                                                                host:
                                                                1883
                                                                (LISTEN)
```

```
# kill 831
```

```
# mosquitto -c /etc/mosquitto/conf.d/broker.conf -v >
mosquitto.log &
```

The preceding command redirects the output to the mosquitto.log file. This way, we can check the log at any time by typing the following command:

```
# cat mosquitto.log
```

Or monitor the log live with

```
# tail -f mosquitto.log
```

Now that we have enabled another new port for secure MQTT communication, we enable it through the firewall as well.

```
# ufw allow 8883
```

Output

```
Rule added
Rule added (v6)
```

A completely modified broker.conf file can be downloaded from the GitHub repository.

Summary

In this chapter, we discussed the message broker in detail and installed and tested one for our own IoT platform. At this stage, we have a fully operational cloud instance along with the MQTT message broker. This is going to serve as a robust and secure real-time message broker for our IoT platform.

In the next chapter, we build a few critical components for our platform.

CHAPTER 7

Building the Critical Components

We began our IoT platform-building journey with the end in mind. That is, we first conceived what our own IoT platform would be like and its high-level contents (refer to Figure 3-1 in Chapter 3). So far, we have established a fully functional cloud instance and the message broker.

The next logical step is to start building the rest of the of platform's plumbing by adding the required blocks of services. In this chapter, we will

- Create a time-series database

- Update Node-RED with additional nodes

- Create a database listener

- Build a REST API–based message publisher and retriever

Creating a Time-Series Core Database

We know that the time-series database is one of the critical blocks of our IoT platform. We established a general data storage schema for this in an earlier chapter. We will create the table now.

Head over to the browser and access the MySQL interface using phpMyAdmin. The first step is to create a separate database in MySQL. We will call it tSeriesDB. Refer to Figure 7-1 for steps to create new database in MySQL using phpMyAdmin interface.

© Anand Tamboli 2019
A. Tamboli, *Build Your Own IoT Platform*, https://doi.org/10.1007/978-1-4842-4498-2_7

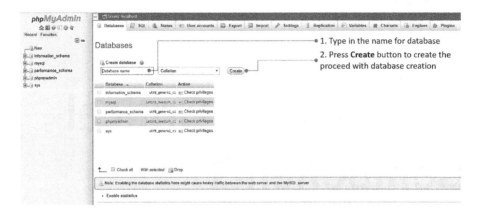

Figure 7-1. *Create a new database for time-series storage*

Next, we create a new user account for the database and assign an appropriate password as shown in Figure 7-2. Adding this user account and access means that every time you or the program wants to access the time-series database, this password will be required.

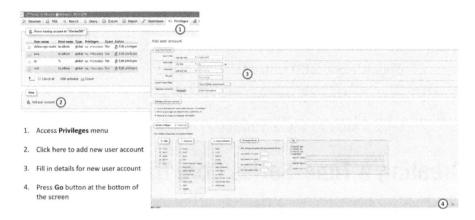

Figure 7-2. *Create new user account for database access*

We now add a data table structure as per the schema mentioned earlier. To add a new table, select the New option under the database name in which this table is to be created (tSeriesDB in this case). Clicking the New option presents a dialog to input a new table name along with several columns.

We could add more or fewer columns at this stage. We can add or remove them later, so just provide an appropriate table name to proceed. We will use the table name thingData for our purpose.

Figure 7-3 explains the data table creation steps in more detail. Notice that we have added one column from the schema. This column is added as a binary type and is called *deleted*. The idea behind this column is to enable us to mark any data point as deleted and thereby discard it from further computations while keeping it there.

We can mark this value as 0 (deleted = 0) when the data point is still valid or active, and mark it as deleted = 1 when we want it to be considered deleted. If we decide to completely remove this value from data storage, then we can delete this row as needed. This provision adds a layer of mistake-proofing for future applications, where it might mistakenly delete an entry. This option enables us to recover records; it can be considered a recycle bin of some kind in our time-series data storage block.

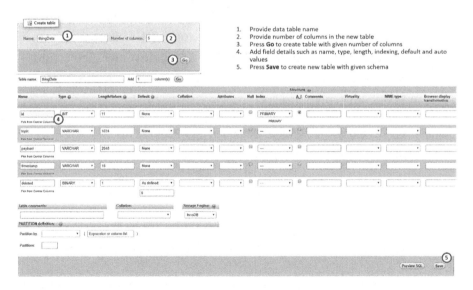

Figure 7-3. *Create data table with designated schema*

Thus, the newly adopted data table schema would like Figure 7-4.

	#	Name	Type	Collation	Attributes	Null	Default	Comments	Extra
☐	1	id 🔑	int(11)			No	*None*		AUTO_INCREMENT
☐	2	topic	varchar(1024)	latin1_swedish_ci		No	*None*		
☐	3	payload	varchar(2048)	latin1_swedish_ci		No	*None*		
☐	4	timestamp	varchar(15)	latin1_swedish_ci		No	*None*		
☐	5	deleted	binary(1)			No			

Figure 7-4. *Updated data table schema for time-series data*

Installing Required Nodes in Node-RED

With the required database and data structure ready in MySQL, it is time to enable Node-RED with the required additional nodes, and then configure it to couple with the database.

The default installation of Node-RED does not have a node to access MySQL. Therefore, we will add this node using Node-RED's *palette manager*.

Open the Node-RED interface in your browser, and then select the Manage Palette option from the menu in the top right. This opens User Settings, and you can type **MySQL** to list the available nodes. Select and install node-red-node-MySQL by following the subsequent prompts. Refer to Figure 7-5 for an explanation.

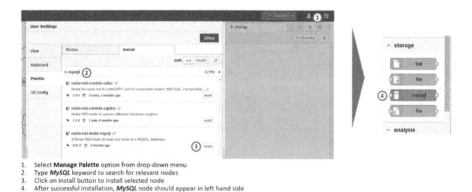

1. Select **Manage Palette** option from drop-down menu
2. Type **MySQL** keyword to search for relevant nodes
3. Click on install button to install selected node
4. After successful installation, **MySQL** node should appear in left hand side palette window

Figure 7-5. *Adding MySQL node to the Node-RED palette*

Having this node available means that now we can access our MySQL database from Node-RED. At this stage, the database and data table are ready to accept and store input values. The Node-RED functional instance is ready for configuration and programming, and the MQTT message broker is functional. This is enough setup to create a database listener and the related APIs.

Creating First Flow for Our Platform

Since the installation of Node-RED, we have not added anything to the node environment. Our canvas is therefore empty. We will create a very basic flow of this at the outset. Let's use inject node for this purpose. The inject node allows us to inject messages into a flow. This could be a default string or a current timestamp. The message can be injected by clicking the button on the node, or we can set a recurring injection by setting a time interval in the node's configuration.

Drag one inject node from the input palette area and place it in the workspace. Now drag a debug node to the workspace area, and then join the two nodes together by connecting an output of the inject node to the debug node. The debug node sends any input given to it on the debug message area on the sidebar on the right-hand side of the window.

The sequence that we just created only exists on our editor screen and is not active. To activate this sequence, press the Deploy button. The flow is deployed and the sequence is now active. If you open the debug sidebar and then press the button on the timestamp flow, you see an output (i.e., current timestamp), in UNIX microsecond format, sent to the debug output. This is a basic and simple flow to start with. Figure 7-6 shows what the sequence looks like, along with some information about the Node-RED editor.

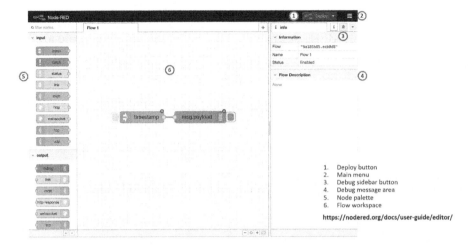

Figure 7-6. *Understanding Node-RED editor and first flow sequence*

Note   For full details on how to use the Node-RED editor, keyboard shortcuts, and various terminologies, refer to the documentation at `https://nodered.org/docs/user-guide/editor/`.

We will make two changes to our basic sequence. The inject node is currently sending a timestamp upon a button press; we will convert this into an autoinject action that repeats itself every 15 seconds. Then, we will add another node from the output palette, mqtt out, to our flow sequence and connect the output of a timestamp inject node to its input.

Adding MQTT Publish Capability

Let's now add an MQTT publish capability in Node-RED. The mqtt out node does not work out of the box; it needs to be configured. We will provide our message broker details and credentials to set this up. Refer to Figure 7-7 for the four steps to set up this sequence. In this configuration, we used port 1883 for connection with the broker; however, remember that we also have secure port 8883 enabled, and we can use that too, if needed. Since we are adding this connection to the same server instance that the broker is installed on, it is not necessary.

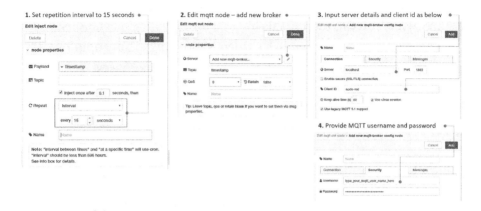

Figure 7-7. *Configure timestamp and MQTT out nodes*

Upon providing all the essential settings, the flow sequence would look like Figure 7-8. After we deploy this sequence, the timestamp injection starts, and it keeps repeating every 15 seconds. The output of the timestamp is sent to two nodes: debug and mqtt out. While debug node shows you the injected timestamp on the debug sidebar, mqtt out pushes this timestamp in the message stream with the timestamp topic and a value of *current UNIX timestamp in microseconds*, something like 1543677926496.

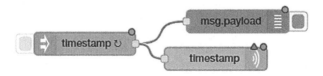

Figure 7-8. *First flow sequence and a timestamp utility for our platform*

111

This flow sequence completes the M1 requirement (publish current timestamp) from the wish list in Chapter 4. Our first flow sequence is doing the same, where we are publishing the current timestamp into the message stream at a fixed interval of 15 seconds. Depending upon the requirements, you can modify this interval to suit your expectations; you can lower it to per second publish (which is too much, in my opinion) or you can raise it to one hour, which is reasonable in most cases.

REST API Message Publisher

Now that we have seen how to publish a message from Node-RED nodes to the MQTT message stream, we will build a REST API to enable the same. Part of our D4 requirement says that devices or applications should be able to publish a message using the HTTP protocol.

To begin, drag the HTTP node from the input block to the workspace. The HTTP node enables us to handle requests from the Web. Once placed in the workspace, double-click the node and modify the node settings, as shown in Figure 7-9. Here we are creating an endpoint as /pub with two parameters passed in the POST request: topic and payload. We can access these parameters in the following nodes as a part of message object: msg. req.params.topic and msg.req.params.payload.

Add another mqtt out node and adjust its settings as shown in Figure 7-9. Note that since we added a broker configuration while creating the timestamp utility, we can simply use the same configuration. We are not specifying the topic in the settings because we will be supplying it in the function node prior to publishing.

Figure 7-9. *Configuration of API nodes and function code*

Now drag two function nodes from the function palette and connect them, as shown in Figure 7-10. Add the HTTP response node at the end of this sequence. This outputs the provided payload as an API response. Remember that it is necessary to have an HTTP response node for every HTTP input node. If not added, the API request will never end and may timeout for the user.

We are not doing any configuration or setting changes for the HTTP output node. Usually, the HTTP output node is only configured if additional headers are sent and configured or the HTTP response code needs to be changed. However, both the headers and the response code can be changed in the previous function node for the HTTP output.

Figure 7-10. *Complete flow sequence for message publish API*

In this flow sequence, two function nodes have code written in them. This code is explained next.

```
// create message
msg.topic = msg.req.params.topic;
msg.payload = msg.req.params.payload;
```

113

```
msg.qos = 2;
msg.retain = false;

return msg;
```

In the `create message` function block, we receive input from the HTTP node. Two parameters, which are passed in the HTTP request, can be accessed in the `msg` message object. In the first two lines, we are assigning input parameters to topic and payload in the main message object. We are also setting the quality of service (QoS) to 2 for better reliability and to retain the flag at false, because we do not want each message to be retained.

These inputs are passed to the mqtt out node, which subsequently publishes a given message payload under the provided topic and with a set QoS of 2 without retaining it on the broker. At the same time, we are responding to the API call by creating a response and sending it with an HTTP response node.

```
// create response
msg.payload = {
    success: true,
    message: "published " +
            msg.req.params.topic +
            "/" +
            msg.req.params.payload
};

return msg;
```

As HTTP response node outputs (i.e., responds to the calling API with payload contents of the message object), we are modifying the payload with two keys. Setting up `success = true` indicates publishing success and payload with a meaningful response message.

Once this is set up and updated, deploy the flow to make it live. If everything is correct, the flow is successfully deployed, and this API is now live. We can test the functionality using cURL, as shown in the following snippet on our Node-RED endpoint.

```
# curl -X POST "https://www.in24hrs.xyz:1880/pub/myTopic/
myPayload" -i
```

Output
```
HTTP/1.1 200 OK
Server: Apache
X-Powered-By: Express
Access-Control-Allow-Origin: *
Content-Type: application/json; charset=utf-8
Content-Length: 56
ETag: W/"38-OoIotXOkbEG/goFLAbvDMSnHdqE"
```

```
{"success":true,"message":"published myTopic/myPayload"}
```

This functionality cannot be tested in web browsers directly because we created a POST API. If you wish to use it in web browsers directly, simply convert it to GET by changing the HTTP input node settings. Alternatively, you can test this functionality using any other utility, such as the Postman interface.

We now have two functionalities added to our IoT platform: first, regular publishing of a current timestamp to the MQTT message stream; second, the REST API for publishing the message to the same MQTT message stream. Let's augment this functionality further by adding the database listener.

Creating the Database Listener

A database listener is essentially an arrangement where a certain program or function listens to the live message stream and stores everything it listens to in the database. In our scenario, we have a live message stream established with MQTT. Now we will build a functionality where our program flow listens to the MQTT stream, and all the messages are logged into the time-series database.

To do this, we will add the mqtt input node to the workspace from the input palette. Then we add the debug node and connect it to the mqtt input node. This is the simplest flow sequence because we literally only have one thing to configure. Note that the MQTT broker details were already added.

In the mqtt input node, we need to provide subscription information and set it to the corresponding broker. To do this, double-click the mqtt input node and configure it, as shown in Figure 7-11. We are subscribing to all the messages with a # subscription and at QoS = 2 for a reliable subscription. Once configured, deploy the flow and monitor the debug messages in the sidebar.

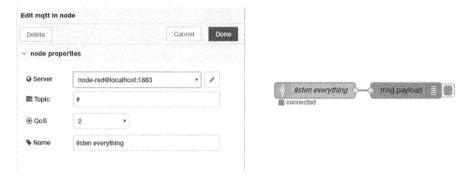

Figure 7-11. *Configure MQTT input node and deploy*

We already have an active timestamp publisher, which is publishing the current timestamp every 15 seconds, and these messages should show up on the debug sidebar every 15 seconds.

Now if we publish any new message with our /pub API, that message will show up on the debug output as well. Once this is verified, let's modify the same flow sequence by adding a function node from the function palette and the MySQL node from the storage palette. Connect these nodes and configure the settings of the MySQL node, as shown in Figure 7-12.

116

Figure 7-12. *Add and configure MySQL node with our time-series database credentials*

The code written in the create query function is explained in the following snippet.

// Create query

```
// get microtime
var timestamp = new Date().getTime()/1000;

// pad it with trailing zeroes
timestamp = timestamp.toString() + "000";

// trim to exact length 10 + 1 + 3
timestamp = timestamp.substring(0, 14);

var strQuery = "INSERT INTO thingData (topic, payload,
            timestamp, deleted) VALUES ('" + escape(msg.
            topic) + "','" + escape(msg.payload) + "','" +
            timestamp + "', 0);";

msg.topic = strQuery;

return msg;
```

117

In the first three lines of the code, we are acquiring the latest timestamp from the date object and converting it to a zero-padded string for storage. The fourth code line is where we are writing our data INSERT query, and it follows standard MySQL insertion syntax.

The MySQL node in Node-RED requires the query to be passed in the msg object as msg.topic. The second-to-last line does that assignment, and then the function returns a modified object to the MySQL node. The MySQL node executes that query and adds the record in the database.

After deploying this flow, we can publish any message using cURL, or simply wait for 15 seconds so that the timestamp is published. Then log in to phpMyAdmin and verify in the database that the new record has been added.

With this flow active, from now on, any message published on the MQTT message stream is recorded in the database. Our database listener is now functional.

REST API Message Retriever

Let's now create an API to retrieve messages stored in the database. In our platform wish list, we have listed two requirements.

- *D1. Get a single data record.* Enables applications and devices to query for a single data record from the time-series data storage based on a specified topic or topic pattern.

- *D2. Get several data records in a series.* Enables applications and devices to query multiple data records based on a specified topic or topic pattern.

Both APIs will be built in almost the same manner as earlier; however, this time, we will use the MySQL node to access and retrieve database values using the SELECT SQL command. Refer to Figure 7-13 for the settings configuration and flow sequence.

Figure 7-13. *Retrieving messages from the time-series data storage*

We have tied the outputs of two HTTP input nodes to the same flow sequence. By doing this, we are accommodating two variations of **/get/**:topic and **/get/**:topic/**last/**:count. The first one retrieves only one message from the time-series database, while with the second one specifies the number of the latest messages to be retrieved.

The following code snippet shows code written for the create query function block.

// Create query

```
// if required record count is not specified
// set default to 1
if(!msg.req.params.count)
    msg.req.params.count = 1;

// build the sql query
msg.topic = "SELECT id,topic,payload,timestamp " +
            "FROM thingData " +
            "WHERE topic='" + escape(msg.req.params.topic) + "' " +
            "AND deleted=0 " +
            "ORDER BY id DESC " +
            "LIMIT " + msg.req.params.count + ";";

return msg;
```

In this code, the first two lines check for the presence of a parameter count. Note that this parameter is required only when we want to request multiple latest messages. Therefore, in a single message query, this parameter is absent. And if it is absent, we set that parameter to the default value of 1.

Then, we are using a standard SELECT query to retrieve database records. In this query, we are using WHERE to search for the specified topic, and deleted=0 to select only the records that were not deleted. Additionally, we are using ORDER BY id DESC to retrieve the latest values and LIMIT the output by using the count parameter.

Since it is a time-series database, and due to the way we built the database listener, all the values are always in a time sequence with latest value on the top (if sorted by ID in descending order). Let's check both APIs now, with cURL first.

```
# curl -X GET "https://www.in24hrs.xyz:1880/get/myTopic" -i
```

Output 1
```
HTTP/1.1 200 OK
Server: Apache
X-Powered-By: Express
Access-Control-Allow-Origin: *
Content-Type: application/json; charset=utf-8
Content-Length: 79
ETag: W/"38-OoIotXOkbEG/goFLAbvDMSnHdqE"

[{"id":8,"topic":"myTopic","payload":"myPayload","timesta
mp":"1543717154.899"}]

# curl -X GET "https://www.in24hrs.xyz:1880/get/myTopic/last/3"
```

Output 2

```
[{"id":8,"topic":"myTopic","payload":"myPayload",
"timestamp":"1543717154.899"},
{"id":7,"topic":"myTopic","payload":"myPayload",
"timestamp":"1543716966.189"},
{"id":6,"topic":"myTopic","payload":"myPayload",
"timestamp":"1543717132.192"}]
```

As these are GET API endpoints, you can test them directly in the browser too. If there are not enough data points (i.e., if you query for five data points under a topic while there are only three in storage, the API will respond to only the three that are available). It will be up to the downstream application to apply appropriate logic in handling such requests.

Verifying that Everything Is Working as Expected

We tested all four core services and utilities as we built them—the recurring current timestamp publisher, the database listener, the HTTP data posting service, and the HTTP data retrieval service.

At this stage, if we publish anything in the MQTT message stream, it will be published live at the same time that the database listener records it in the database. If any message is posted using the HTTP-post service, it will be visible live to MQTT-connected applications and devices (if they are subscribed to that topic). At the same time, this message is recorded in the database. You can retrieve one or more messages from the time-series data storage at any time, without relying on the live connection. All of this can be tested with the command line and a web browser.

Running Node-RED in the Background Continuously

One of the major concerns and an issue that we might encounter is, if the program crashes, we will have to log in to the cloud instance and restart it. That is cumbersome, however, it is more problematic to get to know this situation in first place. This is where, running a service in the background and resurrecting it whenever it fails, or crashes is important.

There are many options to achieve this. We will use one of the suitable options for our type of setup—a utility built using Node.js called *forever*.

The *forever utility* is a simple command-line tool, which is helpful in ensuring that a Node.js-based application runs continuously (i.e., forever). This means that if your application encounters an error and crashes, forever will take care of the issue and restart it for you.

Installation of forever is straightforward and can be achieved with the following command:

```
# npm install forever -g
```

Once installed, we are ready to restart our Node-RED with it. If Node-RED is already running at this stage, you can stop it with the following commands on the command line:

```
# lsof -I :1880
```

Output
```
COMMAND    PID    USER    FD    TYPE DEVICE   SIZE/OFF   NODE   NAME
node-red   1363   root    10u   IPv4 23374         0t0   TCP    *:1880
                                                                (LISTEN)

# kill 1363
```

We see that the Node-RED process was running with ID 1363. We used the `kill` command to stop that process. Now we will run Node-RED with the forever utility, as follows:

```
# forever start -l node-red.log --append /usr/local/bin/node-red
```

In the preceding command, we are starting Node-RED with a log file as `node-red.log`, which means that all the output of the program on the console will go to this file, and we can examine this file as needed.

Now, you can reverify that it is running and that our core APIs are working as expected with the help of the command line and browser testing. The Figure 7-14 shows parts of the block-diagram of our IoT platform that are now functional.

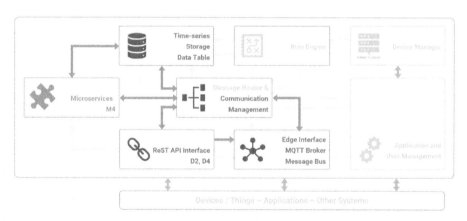

Figure 7-14. *Critical services of our own IoT platform are now functional*

Summary

From what we conceived in the initial chapters, we are about halfway through. We built a created time-series database and added the database listener to the platform. We also created two critical components for the platform in the REST API Interface block.

In the next chapter, we add WebSocket capabilities to our message broker and update access controls for enhanced security. We also see a few examples of how our IoT platform can interface with other applications and systems over MQTT socket connections for live data exchange.

## CHAPTER 8

Configuring the Message Broker

Until now, the message broker and the cloud instance were in a functional state. We added core capabilities to our IoT platform with data access APIs. In this chapter, we modify the configuration of our MQTT broker and make it more useful, especially from an interoperability point of view. In this chapter, we will

- Learn the difference between WebSocket and MQTT

- Learn why WebSocket is important

- Add WebSocket functionality to the broker and test it

- Add access level controls

The Difference Between WebSocket and Normal MQTT

WebSocket provides an always-open communication channel as opposed to a channel with normal HTTP, which opens and closes for each request. WebSocket provides a duplex channel of communication but does not necessarily follow the MQTT protocol. You can have a raw WebSocket implemented and have two devices communicate with it.

MQTT on top of WebSocket adds powerful functionalities. It enables WebSocket clients to choose what they would like to receive, by way of message subscriptions. It also adds a capability to publish a message or information from a client to several other clients via the broker, which in normal circumstances is tedious to implement with basic WebSocket communication. On top of that, additional goodies that come with MQTT make it even better, such as retained messages, QoS, last will and testament (LWT), and so forth.

Why Is WebSocket Important?

From our own IoT platform perspective, it is a fundamental expectation to provide multiple methods to connect the platform to various devices. This is why we selected the HTTP REST interface and MQTT for that purpose. Since both protocols and techniques have their own set of pros and cons, however, being able to combine them provides a significant uplift in the application architecture.

Imagine how your web application can benefit if it is able to communicate live with all the other application users as well as a connected device to the platform. The power it yields to the web application by making it capable of controlling those devices—right from the web browser—is a good reason for enabling WebSocket on MQTT.

Additionally, all systems and things can speak MQTT and/or HTTP and benefit from everything we are incorporating into our IoT platform.

Adding WebSocket to Our MQTT Configuration

Adding WebSocket support to our broker is a straightforward exercise. In the chapter on message brokers, you saw how to add a listener to different ports. We added a local port and a secure port for communication. Now we will add another listener port definition in the configuration file, as follows.

```
# nano /etc/mosquitto/conf.d/broker.conf
```

Update this file with following lines
```
# secure open port for localhost only
listener 1883 localhost

# listen on secure connection with our SSL certificates
listener 8883
certfile /etc/letsencrypt/live/in24hrs.xyz/cert.pem
cafile /etc/letsencrypt/live/in24hrs.xyz/chain.pem
keyfile /etc/letsencrypt/live/in24hrs.xyz/privkey.pem

# listen on secure websocket
listener 8443
protocol websockets
certfile /etc/letsencrypt/live/in24hrs.xyz/cert.pem
keyfile /etc/letsencrypt/live/in24hrs.xyz/privkey.pem
cafile /etc/letsencrypt/live/in24hrs.xyz/fullchain.pem
require_certificate false
tls_version tlsv1.2
```

The first two sections are the same as earlier, adding a local listener and a secure MQTT port. The third section adds a listener on port 8443, and on the next line, it declares this port as following WebSocket. Note that the port number is not standardized for MQTT over WebSocket, so we chose the closest variant that works in most of the network environments—even behind corporate firewalls.

Now that we have enabled another new port for MQTT over WebSocket, we have to enable it through the firewall and then restart the broker to enable new settings.

```
# ufw allow 8443
```

Output

```
Rule added
Rule added (v6)

# pkill mosquitto

# mosquitto -c /etc/mosquitto/mosquitto.conf -v
```

Testing WebSocket

We can now check WebSocket functionality with a publicly available, browser-based MQTT client from the Eclipse Foundation, which can be accessed at www.eclipse.org/paho/clients/js/utility/.

When we open this link, a simple interface, shown in Figure 8-1, opens. Fill in the connection information as shown for our message broker, and then press the Connect button. The Paho browser client connects to our broker, and you can see the new incoming connection log on the command line as the broker is running.

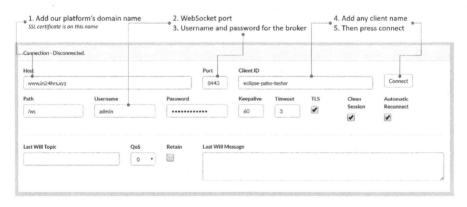

Figure 8-1. *Eclipse Paho utility for testing MQTT WebSocket*

Now subscribe to any topic and try publishing on that topic; you should get the message. You can also try this with our /pub API, so that if you publish something on this API, you see the message appearing on the interface. Similarly, if you publish something from this page, you are able to retrieve the same message from our /get API in the browser. This utility also enables you to publish LWT messages and retained messages. Overall, this client utility can be used for future testing of the platform and MQTT in general.

Additionally, you can download the JavaScript library file from the download section of this utility (or simply view-source and download paho-mqtt.js) from the code. This file is an open source client implementation for WebSocket that can be easily used for your own applications in conjunction with our IoT platform.

Let's Add User Access Controls

When we configured our MQTT broker, we disallowed anonymous logins and thus secured it to a certain level by making it compulsory to provide username-password credentials. However, this does not prevent legitimate users from snooping around in each other's data. Moreover, anyone can publish or receive anything, which is rather unacceptable.

That is why MQTT has another configuration setup known as ACL, or *access control lists.* By using ACLs, we can control access to topics for each user or client. We essentially want to allow only authorized publishers to publish certain topics and authorized subscribers to listen to those broadcasts.

These ACL changes are entirely managed on the broker side, and the client has nothing to do with it at all. To add ACLs on our broker, let's first enable it on our broker. We will modify our broker configuration file, which is located at /etc/mosquitto/conf.d/broker.conf, and add the following line to it in the end. If you are already running the broker on the command line, press Ctrl+C to stop it before editing the file.

```
. . .
acl_file /etc/mosquitto/conf.d/broker.acl
. . .
```

Note that the ACL file name is arbitrary. Once added, save the configuration file and create an actual ACL file in the folder with the following command:

```
# touch /etc/mosquitto/conf.d/broker.acl
```

In general, an ACL file follows a sequence. First, the general access controls the section, followed by user-specific controls, and then pattern-based controls. We will first add the following content to the ACL file, and then discuss the explanation.

```
# nano /etc/mosquitto/conf.d/broker.acl
```

Add following lines to the file
```
# GENERAL
topic read timestamp/#

# USERS
user admin
topic readwrite #

# APPLICATION AS A USER
user my_app_name
topic read timestamp/#
topic readwrite myapp/%c/#

# PATTERNS
topic read timestamp/#
pattern readwrite users/%u/#
pattern write %c/up/#
pattern read %c/dn/#
```

Remember that the broker will treat the entire line as a comment if it starts with #. In the settings, %c and %u are used as wildcard patterns, and each represents a client ID and username, respectively.

The first section is the general settings. Here we have given read rights to general users on the timestamp and its subtopics. Remember that we completely denied anonymous connections on our platform, which means that this section of settings will never be used.

The second section defines settings for two users. The first user has an admin username and read and write access to # (i.e., all the topics). The second user has a my_app_name username and read access to our timestamp topic. Additionally, a full access for read and write is given to the myapp/%c/# topic. This means that any client that connects with a my_app_name username and a unique client ID (e.g., device_1 or similar) is able to read and write on myapp/device_1/#. This way, we can cordon off all the clients within the myapp application domain. Here, no connected client is able to publish on any topic other than the one defined and is only able to subscribe to timestamp.

The last section defines pattern-based settings. Again, we are defining that all clients who do not have the previously mentioned usernames are able to subscribe to the timestamp topic.

Additionally, we are allowing all clients to publish or subscribe on their user-specific topic defined by the users/%u/# pattern, which allows them to write or publish on %c/up/# and subscribe or read on %c/dn/#. This means that if a client with ID device_1 connects with the foo_bar username, then it is able to publish and subscribe on users/foo_bar/#, to publish on device_1/up/#, and to subscribe to device_1/dn/#. Any other publication or subscription that does not match the given pattern will not be honored.

The username-password combination can be reused by multiple applications and/or things; therefore, any changes to user settings would affect all of them. In general, the client ID must be unique when connecting to the broker. Therefore, any access controls in the pattern settings that are based on the client ID apply to only that single client.

Once the ACL file is updated, save and close it. Then create all the user profiles that have been included in the ACL file using the mosquitto_ passwd utility.

Note   Topic names, usernames, and client names are generally case sensitive; not just in ACLs but in the overall MQTT paradigm, things are case sensitive.

To put the ACL into effect, we must restart the broker. We will first terminate the existing process, and then restart with the following commands.

```
# pkill mosquitto

# mosquitto -c /etc/mosquitto/mosquitto.conf -v &
```

Let's Check If This Is Working

It is handy to have a local MQTT client installed on your PC for this testing. There are many options to choose from, including MQTT-FX and MQTTlense. You can search for appropriate programs based on your local machine/PC setup.

Since we already have enabled WebSocket, you can also test this with WebSocket-based clients, such as the Paho utility.

With no ACL in use, we are free to subscribe and publish to any topic. If ACLs are active, the broker will follow the access listed in ACL.

When we connect with the admin username, we are able to subscribe and publish on any topic. This is because we have granted all access to the admin user. However, if we connect with the my_app_name username and try to publish any message, the broker will not publish the message unless it follows the allowed topic pattern as per the ACL.

When denied due to ACL restrictions, there is no way a client would know that the broker denied publishing their message. However, we can see it in the broker log, as shown in Figure 8-2.

```
1543991870: RECEIVED PUBACK from SQC.8883 (Mid: 6654)
1543991880: Received SUBSCRIBE from 1btn/wss
1543991880:     # (QoS 1)
1543991880: 1btn/wss 1 #
1543991880: Sending SUBACK to 1btn/wss
1543991880: Sending PUBLISH to SQC.8883 (d0, q2, r0, m6655, '$SYS/broker/log/M/subscribe', ... (24 bytes))
1543991880: Received PUBREC from $QC.8883 (Mid: 6655)
1543991880: Sending PUBREL to $QC.8883 (Mid: 6655)
1543991880: Received PUBCOMP from $QC.8883 (Mid: 6655)
1543991887: Denied PUBLISH from 1btn/wss (d0, q1, r0, m1, 'test', ... (3 bytes))
1543991887: Sending PUBACK to 1btn/wss (Mid: 1)
1543991887: Sending PUBLISH to $QC.8883 (d0, q2, r0, m6656, '$SYS/broker/clients/total'    (1 bytes))
```

Figure 8-2. *Broker denies the publish based on ACL settings but sends PUBACK = publish an acknowledgment*

Note   For MQTT version 3.1.1, there is no way to inform the client of failure or denial to publish by the broker. This is changing with MQTT version 5.0, in which clients will know that the broker did not publish their message and the reason why.

The pattern settings and the general settings are additive in nature. This means that if the pattern settings do not allow an operation, but the general settings do, then the broker will allow it.

Pattern settings override user settings. Therefore, if the pattern settings allow a client to publish/subscribe to a topic, then the broker will allow it, regardless of the user settings.

Since we have a mandatory username-password requirement when connecting to the message broker, the following scenarios could occur.

- Scenario 1

  - General settings = blank or configured

  - User settings = blank

  - Pattern settings = blank

  - The result is access to all topics denied.

- Scenario 2

    - General settings = blank or configured

    - User settings = configured

    - Pattern settings = blank

    - The result depends on the user settings; the broker ignores general settings.

- Scenario 3

    - General settings = blank or configured

    - User settings = blank or configured

    - Pattern settings = configured

    - The result is pattern settings override user settings.

Using the Forever Tool with the Message Broker

We are using the forever utility to keep Node-RED up and running. We now enable our message broker to do so. This way, if the broker goes down, the forever application will bring it up. While forever can work easily with Node.js-based applications, using it for the Mosquitto broker means additional work is needed.

First, we create a shell script that invokes the mosquitto command, and then we execute that file with the forever tool. Create a shell script with the following commands:

```
# nano mqtt-sh.sh
```

Add following lines to the file
```
#!/bin/sh
/usr/sbin/mosquitto -c /etc/mosquitto/conf.d/broker.conf
```

Once we save this file, let's make it executable and then run it (kill the previous process first) with the forever tool, as follows:

```
# chmod +x mqtt-sh.sh
```

```
# pkill mosquitto
```

```
# forever start -l mqtt.log --append -c -sh /root/mqtt-sh.sh
```

This command starts our message broker in the background and keeps it running forever. All the output from the broker is available in the mqtt. log file for review. To check how many applications are running currently with the forever tool, type **forever list;** in the command line, which gives a list of all the applications running and their uptime and other information.

Summary

Now we have a fully functional MQTT message broker and a partially functional REST API, a working time-series storage, and some utility functions.

In the next chapter, we create the remaining REST APIs and add a message router to the platform. We also add utility APIs to the platform to make it fully ready.

CHAPTER 9

Creating a REST Interface

Since we are ready with the foundation for building meaningful APIs on top of it, in this chapter, we will

- Create data access APIs
- Develop utility APIs

Data Access APIs

As a part of the wish list, we had requirements labeled D1 and D2, which were primarily for accessing data records from the time-series data storage. We covered this when creating core services in Chapter 7. We also covered the D4 requirement for message publishing APIs over HTTP.

The next API that we will create helps us get one or several data records based on a specified condition for topic or payload, or both. This condition can be a topic or payload pattern, and be timestamp dependent, such as needing data for a particular period of time.

All of our data access APIs have a similar structure; each has an HTTP input node `create query` functional block followed by a MySQL node. The output of the MySQL query will go through a prepare response functional node, and then we will send the output through an HTTP response.

© Anand Tamboli 2019
A. Tamboli, *Build Your Own IoT Platform*, https://doi.org/10.1007/978-1-4842-4498-2_9

Each HTTP input node has a unique endpoint structure and method assigned, which can be used in an API call to invoke that sequence of flow. In the create query node, we will build an appropriate query to fetch the data requested, and pass it to the MySQL node, which does the actual querying work. In the prepare response node, we have nothing for now, but then we can add some type of formatting or add a few more objects in the response JSON for augmenting the API functionality further. Figure 9-1 shows what our condition-based data access API looks like.

Figure 9-1. *Condition-based data request API sequence*

Here our endpoint is **/get/topicLike/**:topic/**payloadLike/**:payload/**last/**:count, where the topic and payload inputs are wildcard based. Since we are querying an indefinite number of records, we are making it compulsory to add the number of records requested with the count parameter.

The following code snippet shows code written for the create query function block.

// Create query

```
// if no authentication filter defined or available
// set the default value as 1
if(!msg.req.authFilter)
    msg.req.authFilter = 1;

// wildcard used for API query is * and this needs to be
// converted into SQL wildcard character %
msg.topic = "SELECT id,topic,payload,timestamp" +
            " FROM thingData WHERE" +
            " topic LIKE '" + msg.req.params.topic.
            replace(/\*/g, "%") + "'" +
            " AND" +
```

```
    " payload LIKE '" + msg.req.params.payload.
    replace(/\*/g, "%") + "'" +
    " AND deleted=0" +
    " AND (" + msg.req.authFilter + ")" +
    " ORDER BY ID DESC" +
    " LIMIT " + msg.req.params.count + ";";

return msg;
```

In the preceding code, the first two lines are of critical importance. Although we are not doing it until the end of this chapter, we are preparing our code to be adaptable for authentication filtering. We check if the authFilter object is available, and if it is not available (i.e., its value is not set), we set it to the default value of 1 for now. Setting this to 1 ensures that our code and API will work until we add authentication functionality. In an ideal scenario, this should be set to default 0, so that there will not be any data returned if authFilter is not set.

In the query that we are building later, we replace wildcard character * with an actual SQL wildcard character, which is %. We are deliberately not using % in the API query to avoid it mixing with HTML encoding that might happen in upstream applications. And we are using * as a wildcard because most of the typical topics or payloads do not have that character in common.

However, if you are building your IoT platform for a certain domain-specific application, you could easily change it to suit your requirements. Just remember to change it appropriately wherever we have used it in our code.

In the rest of the query, we also check for non-deleted records. Notice the other condition that we have added with authFilter. In the scenario where no authFilter is provided, the default value is 1. That part of the condition looks like AND (1), which in a SQL sense would simply mean true, and thus would not change the rest of the query. If that value becomes zero, this makes the condition AND (0), and thus would mean

false in SQL. That would essentially negate the rest of the conditions so
that there will be no output.

It is important to note that authFilter does not necessarily hold only
1 or 0; it can very well have another SQL condition that will then combine
with the rest of the query to provide meaningful output. In later stages, we
will replace authFilter with an auth-based query pattern.

Now this query will produce all the records matching our criteria and
limit the output for the record count that we asked for, and then send
it in a JSON response to the API caller. The following is the call to this API
using cURL.

```
# curl -X GET "https://www.in24hrs.xyz:1880/get/topicLike/my*/
payloadLike/*/last/5"
```

Output 1

```
[{"id":18,"topic":"mytopic","payload":"myplayload",
"timestamp":"1543731089.784"},
{"id":8,"topic":"myTopic","payload":"myPayload",
"timestamp":"1543717154.899"},
{"id":7,"topic":"myTopic","payload":"myPayload",
"timestamp":"1543716966.189"}]
```

```
# curl -X GET "https://www.in24hrs.xyz:1880/get/topicLike/
timesta*/payloadLike/*/last/2"
```

Output 2

```
[{"id":31,"topic":"timestamp","payload":"1544011400243",
"timestamp":"1544011400.245"},
{"id":30,"topic":"timestamp","payload":"1544011399074",
"timestamp":"1544011399.078"}]
```

```
# curl -X GET "https://www.in24hrs.xyz:1880/get/topicLike/
timesta*/payloadLike/*88*/last/2"
```

Output 3

```
[{"id":28,"topic":"timestamp","payload":"1544011288907",
"timestamp":"1544011288.910"}]
```

In output 3, notice that although we had 2 in the request count, the response was only one data record because there would have been only one record that was matching our topic and payload pattern requirement. This is the same case with output 1 as well.

Adding Time-Based Filters

In addition to the pattern-based data APIs, we will add time-based APIs. Here we create three endpoints: one for getting records on the specified topic or topic pattern created after the specified timestamp, one for records created before the specified timestamp, and one for records created between the two timestamps.

The flow sequence for this is shown in Figure 9-2.

Figure 9-2. *Time-based data request API sequence*

We have three endpoints here.

- **/get/**:topic/**after/**:time/**last/**:count. topic is the topic name of the data records to be searched. The time parameter is the timestamp in UNIX style for search criteria. We will search for records that were created after this timestamp. And since there could be multiple records that satisfy this criterion, we are making it compulsory to add a number of records requested with the count parameter.

141

- **/get/**:topic/**before/**:time/**last/**:count. The same
  endpoint as after the query, but here we search for
  records created before the timestamp specified.

- **/get/**:topic/**during/**:start/:end/**last/**:count. Here
  we are providing starting and ending timestamps to
  search records created during the timestamps.

Accordingly, based on the endpoint used, the create query function
block is slightly different because the query is different for each. All three
code snippets are shown next.

// Create 'AFTER' query

```
// if no authentication filter defined or available
// set the default value as 1
if(!msg.req.authFilter)
    msg.req.authFilter = 1;

// wildcard used for API query is * and this needs to be
converted into SQL wildcard character %
msg.topic = "SELECT id,topic,payload,timestamp" +
            " FROM thingData WHERE" +
            " topic LIKE '" + msg.req.params.topic.
            replace(/\*/g, "%") + "'" +
            " AND" +
            " timestamp >= '" + msg.req.params.time +  "'" +
            " AND deleted=0" +
            " AND (" + msg.req.authFilter + ")" +
            " ORDER BY ID DESC" +
            " LIMIT " + msg.req.params.count + ";";

return msg;
```

// Create 'BEFORE' query

```
// if no authentication filter defined or available
// set the default value as 1
if(!msg.req.authFilter)
    msg.req.authFilter = 1;

// wildcard used for API query is * and this needs to be
converted into SQL wildcard character %
msg.topic = "SELECT id,topic,payload,timestamp" +
            " FROM thingData WHERE" +
            " topic LIKE '" + msg.req.params.topic.
            replace(/\*/g, "%") + "'" +
            " AND" +
            " timestamp <= '" + msg.req.params.time + "'" +
            " AND deleted=0" +
            " AND (" + msg.req.authFilter + ")" +
            " ORDER BY ID DESC" +
            " LIMIT " + msg.req.params.count + ";";

return msg;
```

// Create 'DURING' query

```
// if no authentication filter defined or available
// set the default value as 1
if(!msg.req.authFilter)
    msg.req.authFilter = 1;

// wildcard used for API query is * and this needs to be
converted into SQL wildcard character %
msg.topic = "SELECT id,topic,payload,timestamp" +
            " FROM thingData WHERE" +
            " topic LIKE '" + msg.req.params.topic.
            replace(/\*/g, "%") + "'" +
            " AND" +
```

```
    " timestamp >= '" + msg.req.params.start + "'" +
    " AND" +
    " timestamp <='" + msg.req.params.end +  "'" +
    " AND deleted=0" +
    " AND (" + msg.req.authFilter + ")" +
    " ORDER BY ID DESC" +
    " LIMIT " + msg.req.params.count + ";";
```

```
return msg;
```

In the preceding three code snippets, everything is the same except one part of the query, where we are adding a condition to check for the timestamps. The query is self-explanatory since it searches for timestamps with less-than or greater-than conditions.

We are using a common block for the output sequence because all the endpoints are of a similar nature. The following cURL-based tests show how the API can be used. Remember that you can also test these APIs in a web browser.

```
# curl -X GET "https://www.in24hrs.xyz:1880/get/mytopic/last/7"
```

Output 1
```
[{"id":18,"topic":"mytopic","payload":"myplayload",
"timestamp":"1543731089.784"},
{"id":8,"topic":"myTopic","payload":"myPayload",
"timestamp":"1543717154.899"},
{"id":7,"topic":"myTopic","payload":"myPayload",
"timestamp":"1543716966.189"}]
```

```
# curl -X GET "https://www.in24hrs.xyz:1880/get/mytopic/before/
1543717154.899/last/5"
```

Output 2

```
[{"id":8,"topic":"myTopic","payload":"myPayload",
"timestamp":"1543717154.899"},
{"id":7,"topic":"myTopic","payload":"myPayload",
"timestamp":"1543716966.189"}]
```

```
# curl -X GET "https://www.in24hrs.xyz:1880/get/mytopic/after/
1543717154.899/last/5"
```

Output 3

```
[{"id":18,"topic":"mytopic","payload":"myplayload",
"timestamp":"1543731089.784"},
{"id":8,"topic":"myTopic","payload":"myPayload",
"timestamp":"1543717154.899"}]
```

```
# curl -X GET "https://www.in24hrs.xyz:1880/get/mytopic/during/
1543717154/1543731089/last/5"
```

Output 4

```
[{"id":8,"topic":"myTopic","payload":"myPayload",
"timestamp":"1543717154.899"}]
```

In the preceding test outputs, the first output is for listing all the available records under the mytopic topic. As you can see, there are only three available. The next three outputs demonstrate how each API is called and its output.

Data Deletion APIs

We will achieve data deletion in two distinct manners. One is recoverable while the other is not. For recoverable deletions, we will use the deleted data table field. For all the queries, we have always searched for deleted=0 in the condition. Now, all we must do is set deleted=1 whenever we want a record to be marked as deleted. It's that simple.

Let's create an API that caters to the following requirements.

- *D5*. Delete a single data record.

- *D6*. Delete several data records in a series.

- *D7*. Delete one or several records based on certain conditions.

The flow sequence for this is shown in Figure 9-3, where we have created four API endpoints.

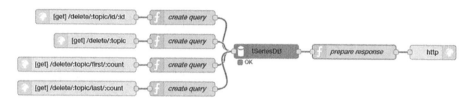

Figure 9-3. *Delete API sequence*

The first endpoint is **/delete/**:topic/**id/**:id, where the topic is a topic name that we are referring to. id is the record ID of the topic record that is to be deleted. You must have seen that every time we published or requested data, it is always returned with id and contents; that is, the id we are referring to here in the API. The following snippet shows the create query block for this endpoint.

```
// if no authentication filter defined or available
// set the default value as 1
if(!msg.req.authFilter)
    msg.req.authFilter = 1;

msg.topic = "UPDATE thingData" +
            " SET deleted=1" +
            " WHERE" +
```

```
" topic='" + msg.req.params.topic + "'" +
" AND (" + msg.req.authFilter + ")" +
" AND id=" + msg.req.params.id + ";";
```

```
return msg;
```

In the preceding snippet, note how we are updating the record that matches a given topic and relevant ID and setting the deleted flag to 1. Note that we are keeping the record in time-series data storage and if needed, you can write another API to undelete the record in the same way, but this time, you set deleted=0 to do so.

The following snippet shows how we are handling **/delete/**:topic API. It is the same as the previous endpoint but with one difference: no specific record ID has been provided.

```
// if no authentication filter defined or available
// set the default value as 1
if(!msg.req.authFilter)
    msg.req.authFilter = 1;
```

```
msg.topic = "UPDATE thingData" +
            " SET deleted=1 " +
            " WHERE" +
            " topic='" + msg.req.params.topic + "'" +
            " AND (" + msg.req.authFilter + ");";
```

```
return msg;
```

In the preceding code, we are marking all the records of the given topic as deleted instead of marking just one. This is a bulk delete API. This time, we will also modify the prepare response function node. For queries other than SELECT, the MySQL node returns different output values. We do not need all of those values because only two are for our direct use for the API.

// Prepare response

```
msg.payload = {
    "found": msg.payload.affectedRows,
    "changed": msg.payload.changedRows,
};
```

```
return msg;
```

In the preceding code, affectedRows is the count of rows that matched the query criterion, while changedRows is the count of rows that were changed with new data. We will now try this API with cURL.

```
# curl -X GET "https://www.in24hrs.xyz:1880/get/timestamp/last/5"
```

Output 1

```
[{"id":36,"topic":"timestamp","payload":"1544188856526",
"timestamp":"1544188856.529"},
{"id":35,"topic":"timestamp","payload":"1544188710842",
"timestamp":"1544188710.845"},
{"id":34,"topic":"timestamp","payload":"1544188664410",
"timestamp":"1544188664.413"},
{"id":33,"topic":"timestamp","payload":"1544188641076",
"timestamp":"1544188641.084"},
{"id":32,"topic":"timestamp","payload":"1544177423967",
"timestamp":"1544177423.973"}]
```

```
# curl -X GET "https://www.in24hrs.xyz:1880
/delete/timestamp/id/34"
```

Output 2

```
{"found":1,"changed":1}
```

```
# curl -X GET "https://www.in24hrs.xyz:1880/get/timestamp/last/5"
```

Output 3

```
[{"id":36,"topic":"timestamp","payload":"1544188856526",
"timestamp":"1544188856.529"},
{"id":35,"topic":"timestamp","payload":"1544188710842",
"timestamp":"1544188710.845"},
{"id":33,"topic":"timestamp","payload":"1544188641076",
"timestamp":"1544188641.084"},
{"id":31,"topic":"timestamp","payload":"1544011400243",
"timestamp":"1544011400.245"},
{"id":30,"topic":"timestamp","payload":"1544011399074",
"timestamp":"1544011399.078"}]
```

As you can see in the preceding three commands, with the first command, we are checking the available records. Note that we have timestamp data from ID 32 to 36. In the second command, we are deleting a record with ID 34. In the third command, we are again checking the last five records. In output 3, we can see that ID 34 is not returned.

The last two endpoints are for deleting the specified count of records from the beginning of the record set or from the end of it. The API is **/delete/**:topic/**last/**:count for deleting a specified number of the latest data records. **/delete/**:topic/**first/**:count is for deleting a specified number of records from the beginning of the record set for the specified topic.

```
// if required record count is not specified
// set default to 1
if(!msg.req.params.count)
    msg.req.params.count = 1;

// if no authentication filter defined or available
// set the default value as 1
if(!msg.req.authFilter)
    msg.req.authFilter = 1;
```

```
msg.topic = "DELETE thingData" +
            " WHERE deleted=1" +
            " AND" +
            " topic='" + msg.req.params.topic + "'" +
            " AND (" + msg.req.authFilter + ")" +
            " ORDER BY id DESC LIMIT " + msg.req.params.count +
            ";";

return msg;
```

The preceding snippet is for deleting the latest count of records. The code for another API is the same, but instead of ordering records in descending order with DESC, we use an ascending order with ASC. For all the operations, you can check in time-series data storage; these records are still there, however, they have the deleted flag set to 1.

These two APIs are useful if you want to implement regular removal of stored data that is old; a delete-first-few API could be handy.

Removing Data Records Completely

What if we want to completely remove the data from the time-series data storage? This is where we create another set of APIs like the delete API. We can call it *purge API*. Figure 9-4 shows the created sequence.

Figure 9-4. *Purge API sequence*

While the endpoints are created to follow the same syntax, the code is slightly different. The following is the code snippet for the first endpoint.

```
// if no authentication filter defined or available
// set the default value as 1
if(!msg.req.authFilter)
    msg.req.authFilter = 1;

msg.topic = "DELETE thingData" +
            " WHERE deleted=1" +
            " AND" +
            " topic='" + msg.req.params.topic + "'" +
            " AND (" + msg.req.authFilter + ")" +
            " AND id=" + msg.req.params.id + ";";

return msg;
```

Notice how we are using a DELETE query. Here we are checking for a specified topic and ID, and whether the deleted status is set or not. This means that we cannot purge the record if it is not deleted. To completely remove a data record from time-series storage, we need two consecutive operations: *delete* followed by a *purge*.

// Purge several records

```
// if no authentication filter defined or available
// set the default value as 1
if(!msg.req.authFilter)
    msg.req.authFilter = 1;

msg.topic = "DELETE thingData" +
            " WHERE deleted=1" +
            " AND" +
            " topic='" + msg.req.params.topic + "'" +
            " AND (" + msg.req.authFilter + ");";

return msg;
```

// Purge first few records

```
// if required record count is not specified
// set default to 1
if(!msg.req.params.count)
    msg.req.params.count = 1;

// if no authentication filter defined or available
// set the default value as 1
if(!msg.req.authFilter)
    msg.req.authFilter = 1;

msg.topic = "DELETE thingData" +
            " WHERE deleted=1" +
            " AND" +
            " topic='" + msg.req.params.topic + "'" +
            " AND (" + msg.req.authFilter + ")" +
            " ORDER BY id ASC LIMIT " + msg.req.params.count +
            ";";
return msg;
```

A query to purge the last few records is similar to that for the first few, except the ordering keyword must be changed from ASC to DESC.

For now, we have completed the data API as per our wish list. There are still many areas for improvement, which can further strengthen the API while keeping it simple and straightforward. We will review these aspects later.

Adding Microservices to the Platform

Microservices are non-structured functionalities that are used by applications and devices alike. We listed seven microservices on our platform wish list. Now we will build all of them.

Getting the Current Timestamp

We built a current timestamp publishing service in the previous chapter, which fulfills requirement M1. We will now add a polling-based timestamp service. It will be a simple API, as shown in Figure 9-5. For the devices or applications that missed the latest timestamp broadcast and cannot wait until the next broadcast, this service is quite useful. With this microservice availability, you can also force an application or device to update its clock based on a random timestamp request.

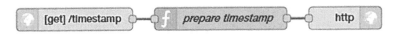

Figure 9-5. *Microservice to request a current timestamp*

This is the simplest API we have on our IoT platform. It can be accessed on the /timestamp endpoint. The prepare timestamp function node has only a few lines of code, as follows.

```
msg.payload = {
    timestamp: (new Date()).getTime().toString()
};

return msg;
```

We are creating a new date object, converting it into a UNIX-styled timestamp, and then formatting it as a string before packing it into a message object.

```
# curl -X GET "https://www.in24hrs.xyz:1880/timestamp"
```

Output
```
{"timestamp":"1544201700375"}
```

A quick command-line test using cURL shows the output in a UNIX-styled microsecond timestamp.

153

Random Code Generator

Let's create another quick utility to generate a random alphanumeric string of a given length. This is a particularly handy service for creating tokens, default passwords, or API keys. Figure 9-6 shows the sequence for this service.

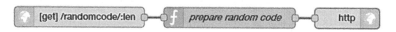

Figure 9-6. *Microservice to request random code of a specified length*

The code snippet for the prepare random code function node is shown next.

```
var randomString = function(length) {
    var text = "";
    var possible = "ABCDEFGHIJKLMNOPQRSTUVWXYZabcdefghijklmnopq
                rstuvwxyz0123456789";

    for(var i = 0; i < length; i++) {
        text += possible.charAt(Math.floor(Math.random() *
        possible.length));
    }

    return text;
}

msg.payload = {
        code: randomString(msg.req.params.len)
    };

return msg;
```

We first defined a function that can generate a random string of a given length. After the function definition, we simply pass the output of this function to the message object and send it through as an output. The command-line testing for this API is shown next.

```
# curl -X GET "https://www.in24hrs.xyz:1880/randomcode/32"
```

Output 1
```
{"code":"ASQ6t9PidHZOBKxIsQfguD72fpODcErq"}
```

```
# curl -X GET "https://www.in24hrs.xyz:1880/randomcode/8"
```

Output 2
```
{"code":"rU5rB3Db"}
```

```
# curl -X GET "https://www.in24hrs.xyz:1880/randomcode/64"
```

Output 3
```
{"code":"bydGpfpth9xE4vy9HcM97s1Jm3dmMipBOUuJB2Lqn95pkPrMM4Idxt
axUEBLvR1A"}
```

As you can see, we are now able to generate random strings of varied sizes. As such, there is no limit on the maximum length of the random string that you can generate; however, typically 32 or 64 bytes are commonly used, and 128 bytes in some cases. It is totally dependent on each use case.

Adding New Modules to Node-RED

Before we create the remaining three microservices, we need to install additional Node-RED modules. These nodes are UUID, Sendgrid (for email service), and Twilio (for the text-messaging service).

To install additional nodes, select the Manage Palette option in the main menu of the Node-RED interface. Click the Install tab and type a search term, **contrib-uuid.** You see a contributed package, node-red-contrib-uuid, as shown in Figure 9-7. Press the Install button to add the node to the node palette.

We search and install `node-red-contrib-sendgrid` and `node-red-node-twilio` the same way (see Figure 9-7). Note that, by default, Node-RED has an email node for sending and receiving emails. You can try using that node too; however, I have seen that it does not offer much customization and can be painful to maintain due to security restrictions by mail accounts and clients. Sendgrid, on the other hand, is an automated email-sending program.

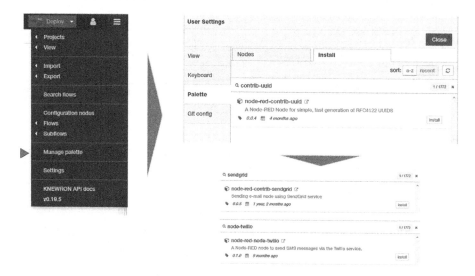

Figure 9-7. *Installing additional nodes from the palette manager*

UUID Generator

Now that we have all the required nodes installed, let's create a UUID generator microservice. The flow sequence for the UUID generation API is shown in Figure 9-8, along with settings for a UUID node.

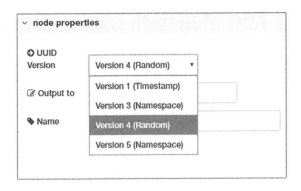

Figure 9-8. *UUID generation node settings and flow sequence*

We have set a UUID node to generate random codes; however, you can also try generating them based on a specific namespace or timestamps. When UUIDs are generated based on a namespace and timestamps, most of the content is nearly the same and follows a certain pattern. UUID node outputs the code in `msg.payload` in string format, which we convert into a message object in a prepare response node, as shown in the following code.

// Prepare response

```
msg.payload = {
    uuid: msg.payload
}

return msg;
```

Let's quickly check the functionality of this API with cURL; the endpoint here is **/uuid**.

```
# curl -X GET "https://www.in24hrs.xyz:1880/uuid"
```

Output

```
{"uuid":"a304fad2-36d1-4fda-9e2d-da820524ce6f"}
```

Email and Text Message Microservice APIs

To use Twilio and Sendgrid, you must have an account with each of them. You can register for a Twilio account at `www.twilio.com` and for a Sendgrid account at `https://sendgrid.com`. When you create an account, you get various credentials. Jot down the credentials safely because you will need them to configure both nodes for the first time (see Figure 9-9).

Configuration of Nodes

To begin, drag both nodes to the workspace from the left-hand side of the Node palette.

Once placed on the workspace canvas, double-click the sendgrid node and provide the API key in its settings window. That is all we need to do to set up the sendgrid node. The rest of the values, such as From and To email addresses, are provided when we build the service. You can name this node if needed; otherwise, it will have the default name, sendgrid.

Now double-click the twilio node and then press the pencil icon to create a Twilio configuration. This opens another dialog box, where three important inputs are needed. Paste your Account SID, Twilio number, and authentication token (as provided on your Twilio account page). You can then assign a name to the config if needed, and click Add to save this config.

This configuration is saved separately and can be used by multiple nodes later. Upon saving this confirmation, you are back on the twilio node settings dialog box. Select this configuration from the drop-down menu (there is only one the first time). No other fields need to be changed because we will change them programmatically later.

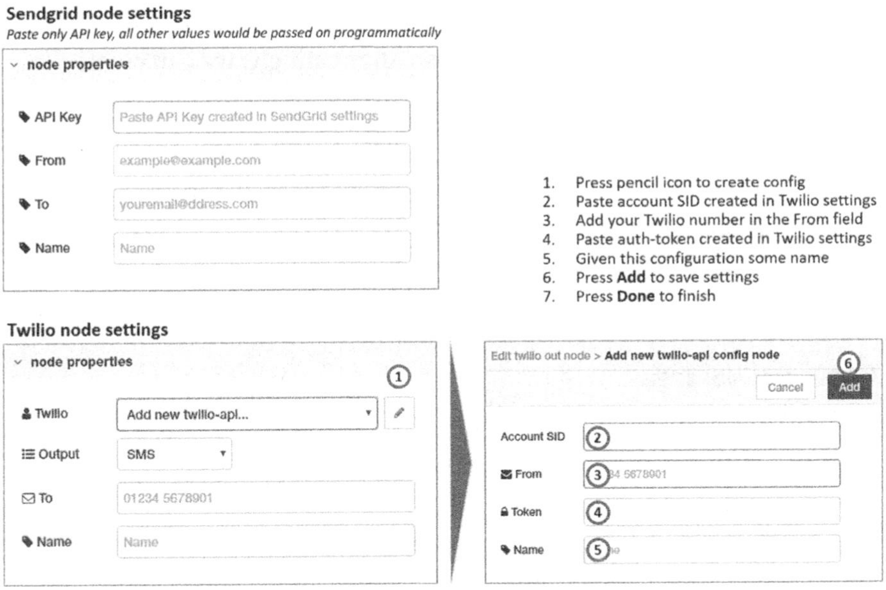

Sendgrid node settings
Paste only API key, all other values would be passed on programmatically

> ⌄ **node properties**
>
> ● API Key | Paste API Key created in SendGrid settings |
>
> ● From | example@example.com |
>
> ● To | youremail@address.com |
>
> ● Name | Name |

1. Press pencil icon to create config
2. Paste account SID created in Twilio settings
3. Add your Twilio number in the From field
4. Paste auth-token created in Twilio settings
5. Given this configuration some name
6. Press **Add** to save settings
7. Press **Done** to finish

Twilio node settings

> ⌄ **node properties**   ①
>
> ▲ Twilio | Add new twilio-api... ▾ | ✎
>
> ☰ Output | SMS ▾ |
>
> ✉ To | 01234 5678901 |
>
> ● Name | Name |

> Edit twilio out node > **Add new twilio-api config node**   ⑥
>
>   Cancel   **Add**
>
> Account SID ② | |
>
> ✉ From   ③ |4 5678901 |
>
> 🔒 Token   ④ | |
>
> ● Name   ⑤ |o |

Figure 9-9. *Node settings for Twilio and Sendgrid nodes*

SMS Sending Utility

With the configuration settings in place, let's create a SMS API with the flow sequence shown in Figure 9-10.

Figure 9-10. *Send text message flow sequence*

Here our endpoint is defined as **/sms/to/**:to/**message/**:message, where to is the target mobile number to which we want to send a text message, and message is the actual body of the text message.

Notice that the twilio node does not have an output, so there is no direct way to know if our SMS sending request was successful. Being asynchronous in nature, Twilio provides callback functionality in its account

159

settings. You can specify a callback URL, which is called upon successful message delivery or upon failure to do so. Interestingly, we can create another API for this purpose and process all the delivery reports as needed by the application. I will leave it to you to explore this option because it is not complex, and it does not form a critical part of the platform.

Accordingly, two function blocks do the processing. The first function prepares the message for dispatch via the twilio node, while the other prepares the HTTP API response. The following shows code for both.

```
// Prepare message
msg.topic = msg.req.params.to;
msg.payload = msg.req.params.message;

return msg;
```

```
// Prepare response
msg.payload = {
    "smsTo": msg.topic,
    "message": msg.payload,
    "status": "queued"
};

return msg;
```

The twilio node needs the target number in the topic part of the message and the message body in the payload. In the prepare message function node, we prepare this message packet as per this requirement.

The prepare response node simply responds to the API caller with the status as queued, along with echoing back what was sent to it. Once deployed, this flow can be checked with the following cURL command and the target mobile should receive a message (Hi) in their SMS inbox.

```
# curl -X GET "https://www.in24hrs.xyz:1880/sms/
to/+1234567890/message/Hi"
```

Output

```
{"smsTo":"+1234567890","message":"Hi","status":"queued"}
```

Email-Sending Utility

Now that our text-messaging API is working as expected, we will create a flow sequence for an email-sending functionality (see Figure 9-11). It is almost like the text-message-sending flow.

Figure 9-11. *Send email flow sequence*

For sending email messages, we have simplified a version of the API with the **/email/to/**:to**/subject/**:subject**/message/**:message endpoint, where the parameters are self-explanatory. The first parameter, to, provides the target email address to which email needs to be sent, followed by the email subject and message body in the message parameter.

The sendgrid node requires inputs to be given in the msg object, and it does not have any output. We are therefore adding a prepare response function that responds to the API caller.

// Prepare email

```
msg.from = "in24hrs <the.author@in24hrs.the.book>";
msg.to = msg.req.params.to;
// msg.cc = "cc_address@example.com";
// msg.bcc = "bcc_address@example.com";
msg.topic = msg.req.params.subject;
msg.payload = msg.req.params.message;

return msg;
```

161

// Prepare response

```
msg.payload = {
    "to": msg.to,
    "status": "email queued"
};
return msg;
```

As shown in the code snippets, the first part is for preparation of email input to the sendgrid node. We are also able to pass Cc and Bcc email addresses to the sendgrid node; however, we have not included them in our API endpoint. Should you need to add them, you can easily extend the API to incorporate those parameters. Additionally, we must provide a valid From email address for this node; in most cases, this should be your application's generic email address, or it could be a do-not-reply address.

I find it useful to provide an existing valid email address in this parameter so that when a receiver responds, there is someone to answer to that email.

If you wish to send larger-size email messages, then perhaps a GET API will not suffice, due to length limitations. In that case, you can easily convert this API to POST and utilize the increased capacity. Like Twilio, Sendgrid provides a callback URL configuration in its account settings, and you can configure an API where the email-sending status is reported. Various statuses are reported—mainly events such as email sent, delivered, opened, dropped, bounced, blocked, and so forth. This setting is available under the Mail settings in the Event Notification menu on the Sendgrid control panel.

Summary

In this chapter, we built data access APIs, microservices, and required utilities as per our wish list. We have one more microservice to build, which is dependent on the rule engine block's functionality.

The rule engine and authentication are two important components/blocks in our platform, and in the next chapter, we will build them.

CHAPTER 10

Rule Engine and Authentication

The rule engine is one of the most powerful blocks of our IoT platform or any IoT platform in general. The fact that anything happening in the connected environment of an IoT platform can trigger something else to happen makes the rule engine a critical block.

In this chapter, we will

- Establish working logic for our rule engine

- Build the relevant rule engine flow

- Create APIs for rule management

- Understand authentication logic and implement it

Start with the Rule Engine Logic

We can build a rule engine infrastructure in several ways. There is no right or wrong way per se. There is only smart and smarter or efficient or more efficient. At the same time, the value of a rule engine is directly proportional to the simplicity it can provide and the job it can do to achieve the result. If you must build too many things to achieve results, the value of that build starts to diminish.

© Anand Tamboli 2019
A. Tamboli, *Build Your Own IoT Platform*, https://doi.org/10.1007/978-1-4842-4498-2_10

Keeping this in mind, we can build our rule engine in two ways. We can leverage the Node-RED flow-based approach and simply add a message stream listener, which can then distribute messages to several other nodes based on certain preprogrammed criterion, and then take further actions. The keyword here is *preprogrammed*. Yes, that means that we always have to manually preprogram the rules before deploying them. This makes the approach somewhat rigid. What if we must add a new rule on the fly? Or activate or deactivate an existing rule based on another rule's output? These scenarios lead us to another approach: query-based rules. And this is what we will build now.

Creating a Database

The first step in building a query-based rule engine is to define the data schema and add a data table in our time-series data storage. Let's create this rule table, as shown in Figure 10-1.

#	Name	Type	Collation	Attributes	Null	Default	Comments	Extra
1	id 🔑	int(11)			No	*None*		AUTO_INCREMENT
2	ruleName	varchar(255)	latin1_swedish_ci		No	*None*		
3	active	binary(1)			No			
4	topicPattern	varchar(1024)	latin1_swedish_ci		No	*None*		
5	payloadPattern	varchar(2048)	latin1_swedish_ci		No	*None*		
6	method	varchar(7)	latin1_swedish_ci		No	GET		
7	webHook	varchar(1024)	latin1_swedish_ci		No	*None*		

Figure 10-1. *Rule engine data table schema*

We are naming it the `ruleEngine` table. In this data table, we have a primary key and an autoincrementing value, `id`. This is required to refer to any rule going forward. `ruleName` is the readable name of the rule. The `active` column is binary in nature and defines whether the rule is active or not. There are two columns that define a rule's logic: `topicPattern` and payloadPattern. These columns hold SQL-like patterns for rule qualifications; based on their qualifications, we can use the webHook value to call on using a defined method in the method column. By default, method is set to GET request.

There could be several possibilities in which we can use this structure or augment it. We can certainly add a few more columns that can hold various other actions to be executed, values to be changed, scripts to be executed, or other global variables to be affected. We can also do all that in another web service or script file located at the webHook URL. It is cleaner this way.

Once this table is created, a typical entry looks like the one shown in Figure 10-2.

	id	ruleName	active	topicPattern	payloadPattern	method	webHook
Edit Copy Delete	1	timestamp rule	1	timestamp%	%	POST	https://www.in24hrs.xyz:1880/pub/modifiedTime/rule...

Figure 10-2. *Typical rule entry in our ruleEngine table*

Let's look at what we have added to the table. At the outset, we are calling/naming this rule *timestamp rule*, and the same is appearing in the ruleName column. The next field, active, is set to 1, which means the rule is active. If we want to disable this rule, we simply set active to 0. The topicPattern field has a value of timestamp%. The payloadPattern field is %, which is a pattern similar to what you would use for SQL queries. From the rules' perspective, this means that the rule should execute if the received topic matches this pattern (timestamp%) (i.e., the topic starts with the word timestamp) and can have anything after that. For the payload, the pattern is set to % (i.e., anything is acceptable in the payload). The last two fields define the webHook information: the method field defines the type of call, and the webHook field has an actual URL to be invoked.

Building the Flow Sequence

With this sample entry ready, let's create a sequence for in-flow rule execution. Figure 10-3 shows the created sequence.

Note   While we already had a database listener, we have tied our rule sequence to the same listener. This will enable us to execute rules faster and closer to the time of message reception in the message stream.

Figure 10-3. *Rule engine flow sequence in combination with database listener*

Here we have connected the first function block, *search rules,* to the MQTT listener; thus, every time a new message is in the stream, this block will search for corresponding rules. The MySQL node helps fetch those rules from the `ruleEngine` data table. Once we have the rules available, we are invoking webhooks and sending the output of a webhook to the debug node for displaying the output on a debug console.

// Search rules

```
msg.topic = "SELECT * FROM ruleEngine" +
            " WHERE" +
            " ('" + msg.topic + "' LIKE topicPattern)" +
            " AND" +
            " ('" + msg.payload + "' LIKE payloadPattern)" +
            " AND active=1";

return msg;
```

The preceding code snippet shows the code written in the *search rules* block. The query written implements a reverse search technique. In a normal scenario, the query searches for columns matching a pattern; however, in this case, we are searching for a pattern that matches columns. The query also checks for only active rules (i.e., active=1). The call webHook block receives the output of the query and has the following code in it.

// Call webhook

```
if(msg.payload.length !== 0)
{
    for(var i = 0; i < msg.payload.length; i++)
    {
        msg.method = msg.payload[i].method;
        msg.url = msg.payload[i].webHook;

        node.send([msg]);
    }
}
```

The preceding snippet seems slightly unusual because it does not have return msg; code in it. The node first checks the length of the payload and executes a piece of code only if that length is non-zero. If there is no rule matching to the criterion, then the payload is empty, and thus we avoid going further (because there is no return statement after the if clause). However, if there is some payload, it has an array of rule objects. If there are multiple rules matching the rule condition, then there is more than one.

With the for loop, we ensure that all the rules are executed in sequence (i.e., the rule that was first created is executed first). By default, SQL results are in ascending order, which ensures that our rules are executed in the order of creation—the lowest ID executes first.

When we have a rule object, we assign an HTTP calling method and URL to it to be passed on to the HTTP request node. Then we send this packet through using a node.send statement. It forms an input to the HTTP request node, which has the settings shown in Figure 10-4.

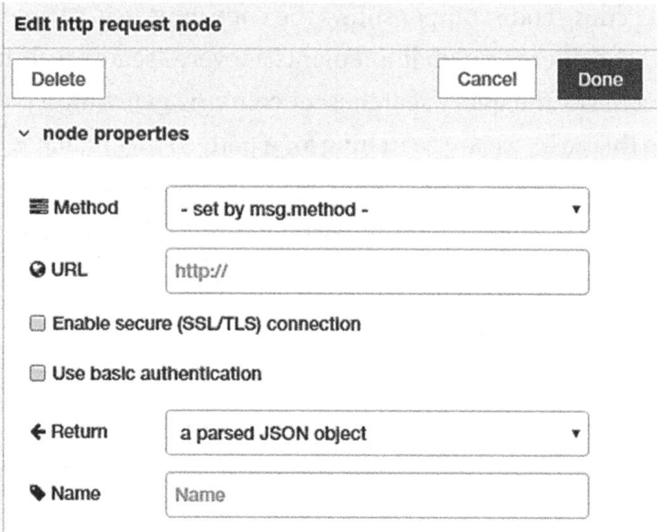

Edit http request node

| Delete | | | | Cancel | Done |

∨ **node properties**

≣ Method | - set by msg.method - ▾ |

◉ URL | http:// |

☐ Enable secure (SSL/TLS) connection

☐ Use basic authentication

← Return | a parsed JSON object ▾ |

❧ Name | Name |

Figure 10-4. HTTP request node configuration

This means that the HTTP request node will execute an HTTP call and return the output as a parsed JSON object, which we are simply sending to the debug output.

At this stage, we have our rule engine flow ready, along with one rule added to the rule table. In Figure 10-5, the webhook that we added is POST (`www.in24hrs.xyz:1880/modifiedTime/rule-engine-works`). This is essentially our own data publish API call, which means that when a rule is executed, the /pub API is called and it publishes another message under the `modifiedTime` topic and the `rule-engine-works` payload.

Testing the Rule Engine

We can test this in several ways, but the best way is to check it with the Paho MQTT utility because you are able to see the action live (i.e., when you publish a timestamp message, it is picked up and the rule engine searches for a rule). Since we already have a matching rule available, it will be executed and another message will be published. While you are on the Paho page, you see this second message coming in live, in almost no time.

To see how powerful our rule engine is, update the `ruleEngine` table with additional rules, as shown in Figure 10-5.

Figure 10-5. *Two rules matching same criterion and one matching subsequent criterion*

Here we have two rules matching the criterion (i.e., rule `id` 1 and `id` 2), whereas when we execute rule 2, it publishes a message, `rule-engine-working-again`. We have configured the third rule not to check `topicPattern` but `payloadPattern` for messages that end with the word `again`. This means that our second rule triggers the third rule.

Check this again in the Paho utility. You should see upon publishing something on the `timestamp` topic; there should be three additional messages following that.

Note   Remember to carefully craft your rules and check for circular references. If not handled carefully, these could result in a loop, which can lock access in no time.

Rule Management APIs

To manage rules easily, we will create three APIs that

- Enable or disable a specified rule by ID

- Enable or disable all the rules at once (handy when you want to stop all rules)

- Create a new rule with the callback (fulfills the M7
  requirement of our wish list)

Enable and Disable a Specific Rule

The first API flow sequence is followed by functional code, as shown in
Figure 10-6.

Figure 10-6. *Activate or deactivate rule flow sequence*

We have created two APIs: **/rules/enable/**:id and **/rules/disable/**:id
for enabling and disabling rules by their ID. These two similar function
blocks for creating a query differ in that one sets the active value to 1 while
the other sets it to 0.

// Create query - /rules/enable/:id

```
msg.action = "enable";

msg.topic = "UPDATE ruleEngine" +
            " SET active=1" +
            " WHERE" +
            " id=" + msg.req.params.id + ";";

return msg;
```

The preceding code snippet is for enabling a query. We are creating
this query and adding one variable to a msg object as action="enable".
This enables us to respond properly in the prepare response functional
block. Accordingly, the prepare response function has the following code.

// Prepare response

```
msg.payload = {
    "status": msg.action + " success"
};

return msg;
```

We are using an action variable from an upstream block to create a meaningful response. Since we already have one rule with id=1 in our table, we can activate or deactivate it with the following cURL.

```
# curl -X GET https://www.in24hrs.xyz:1880/rules/disable/1
```

Output
```
{"status":"disable success}
```

Now if you check the database, the rule has an active=0 value.

Enable and Disable All Rules

The second API that we will create enables or disables all the rules at once. This is a straightforward creation with a minor difference: the query will not check for any id value, so it applies to all the rules. The flow sequence for this API is shown in Figure 10-7.

Figure 10-7. *Activate or deactivate all rules*

// Create query - rules/enableAll

```
msg.action = "enable all";
msg.topic = "UPDATE ruleEngine SET active=1;";

return msg;
```

173

The preceding code snippet that enables all API query code is self-explanatory. The code written for prepare response is the same as the earlier API's.

Create a New Rule

Now we will create the third API to add a new rule. As mentioned earlier, we can use this API to create new rules and to have applications register a callback on the go. The flow sequence is shown in Figure 10-8.

Figure 10-8. *Register a call back (add new rule) flow sequence*

The flow sequence follows a standard pattern and creates an endpoint, **/rules/add/**:rulename, where the balance of the parameters to the API are passed on in the POST body. The first function, create query, then inserts a new rule record in the ruleEngine table. Note that we have set the default value of an active field to 0, which means that when created, the rule will be inactive by default. The code snippets for both create query and prepare response are shown next.

// Create query

```
var ruleName = msg.req.params.rulename;

var topicPattern = msg.req.body.topicPattern;
var payloadPattern = msg.req.body.payloadPattern;
var method = msg.req.body.method;
var webHook = msg.req.body.webHook;

msg.topic = "INSERT INTO ruleEngine (ruleName, topicPAttern,
            payloadPattern, method, webHook)" + " VALUES" +
```

```
            " ('" + ruleName + "', '" + topicPattern + "', '" +
            payloadPattern + "', '" + method + "', '" + webHook + "');";

return msg;
```

// Prepare response

```
if(msg.payload.affectedRows !== 0)
{
    msg.payload = {
        "status": "rule added",
        "ruleName": msg.req.params.rulename,
        "ruleId": msg.payload.insertId
    };
    return msg;
}
```

Once the rule is added to ruleEngine, we send its ID in the response. Upstream applications or devices can use this for further actions on rules. Deploy this flow sequence and then use cURL to test the functionality, as follows.

```
# curl -X POST "https://www.in24hrs.xyz:1880/rules/add/testRule"
--data-urlencode "topicPattern=%stamp"
--data-urlencode "payloadPattern=%1234%"
--data-urlencode "method=GET"
--data-urlencode "webHook=https://www.in24hrs.xyz:1880/sms/
              to/+1234567890/message/pattern detected"
```

Output 1
```
{"status":"rule added","ruleName":"testRule","ruleId":4}
```

```
# curl -X GET https://www.in24hrs.xyz:1880/rules/disable/4
```

Output 2
```
{"status":"enable success}
```

First, we are creating a new rule called `testRule`, which is triggered if the topic is like `%stamp` (which could be `timestamp` or anything else) and the payload has four numbers in sequence (e.g., `%1234%`). When this condition is met, we are setting it to send us an SMS using our SMS API. Before you add this rule, make sure that you have inserted a valid mobile number in place of the dummy one.

Upon successful creation, we get the output and its ID (which is 4 in this case.) Remember that this rule is still inactive, so we use our enable API and enable it. Once our rule is active, head over to the Paho MQTT utility and publish something on the `timestamp` topic. Make sure that the payload has the number sequence 1234 in it (e.g., payload = 1544**31234**0320). If everything is set up correctly thus far, the specified mobile number will receive an SMS that says, "Pattern detected."

We can also create an additional API to delete the rule from `ruleEngine`. It is not explained or demonstrated here; however, you can follow the same logic as in the `/purge` API, and create it yourself.

Building Another Rule Engine with Node-RED

While the rule engine that we are building is using the time-storage database for functioning, we can also build a rule engine with the Node-RED interface. However, as I mentioned earlier, it will not be dynamic in nature and would need to be manually modified every time you want to change rules; at least to a larger extent. Moreover, this method does not check for multiple input parameters (i.e., it can check for topic content or payload content but not both at once). It is the biggest advantage of our core rule engine, which utilizes time-series data storage. For known and fixed rules, however, this serves as an effective and efficient alternative. Let's see how it can be utilized.

Refer to Figure 10-9, which shows a rule engine with the three rules configured; the fourth one is a default value.

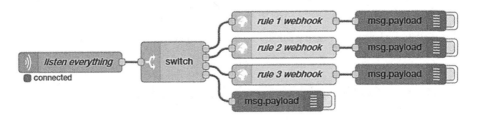

Figure 10-9. *Node-RED-based rule engine*

This construct continuously listens to the message stream and uses a switch node from Node-RED for matching every message with predefined conditions. These conditions could be as simplistic as `if message-payload = something`, to anything complex with regular expressions (a.k.a. RegEx).

I have created two rules to demonstrate how this type of rule engine can work (see Figure 10-5). This method, however, will not allow us to modify these rules programmatically. If this is okay with your type of application or domain, you should use this method because it offers a higher level of ease.

In fact, you can use both constructs together and use an appropriate mix of rules to match needs. This would be an even more powerful implementation than either method alone. The three rules created with this method are shown in Figure 10-10. You will see that their subsequent actions are different from one other.

Figure 10-10. *Rules with Node-RED*

177

You can test this rule engine in the same manner as the earlier one. The debug sidebar in Figure 10-10 shows sample test results.

Adding Authentication to the Data API

In simple terms, *authentication* means confirming your own identity, while *authorization* means granting access to the system. Simply put, with authentication, the system verifies the user, accessing system, or application. With authorization, the system verifies if the requester has access to the requested resource(s).

Since our focus has been on the core of the platform all the while, it would make sense to have some level of built-in authentication abilities. It would be ideally handled by an upstream application. It would make sense to add *topic-based* access control to the data access API. We will follow the same logic that we used while adding access controls to the MQTT broker configuration.

What Are Our Options?

There are several authentication and authorization methods, and many systems utilize customizations of a few major approaches. The following are three popular approaches.

- *Basic.* With HTTP basic authentication, the user agent provides a username and password to prove their authenticity. This approach does not require cookies, sessions, or logins, and so forth. Information is provided in the HTTP header. As many experts would suggest, the biggest issue with *basic* authentication is that unless the SSL is fully enforced for security, the authentication is transmitted in open and insecure channels, and thus is rendered useless. The username and password combination are encoded in the *base64* format before adding to the header. In general, this option is good at balancing system costs and performance.

- *API key*. This was created as somewhat of a fix to basic authentication and is a relatively faster approach. A uniquely generated random value or code is assigned to each user for authentication, and usually, such a string is long enough to be guessed easily. Additionally, setting up this type of system is relatively easy, and controlling these keys, once generated, is even easier since they can be managed fully from the server side. While this method *is better* than a *basic* authentication method, it is *not the best.*

- *OAuth*. OAuth combines authentication and authorization to allow more sophisticated scope and validity control. However, it involves an authentication server, a user, and the system to do the handshake, and thereby perform authentication, which leads to authorization. This is supposedly a stronger implementation from a security perspective; however, it is also a time-consuming and costly proposition. Does this fit your purpose? It depends upon what do you plan to do!

Note   In general, the use of the API key method provides the best compromise between implementation costs, ease of usage, and performance overhead. We will use the API key method for authentication. I prefer to keep things as simple as possible, because every time you make the solution unnecessarily complex, you are also likely to leave a hole in it.

In our implementation, we are using authentication only for data access APIs because that is the critical piece of currency our platform may hold. When you implement your own platform, you can take the lead from this implementation and extend it to all other APIs as you see fit.

What Is the Plan?

To implement a simplified API, key-based authentication, and access control, we will make use of another data table in the time-series database, which can hold API keys and relevant information for our use. We then ensure that every time an API call is received for a data request, we check a supplied key and assert access controls via modification of our base queries. In previous chapters, we provisioned most of the APIs for this usage in the form of `authFilter`. The minimally required data schema for `authTable` is shown in Figure 10-11.

#	Name	Type	Collation	Attributes	Null	Default	Comments	Extra
1	id	int(11)			No	None		AUTO_INCREMENT
2	user	text	latin1_swedish_ci		No	None		
3	token	varchar(1024)	latin1_swedish_ci		No	None		
4	access	varchar(4096)	latin1_swedish_ci		No	0		
5	details	varchar(1024)	latin1_swedish_ci		No	None		
6	last_change	timestamp		on update CURRENT_TIMESTAMP	No	CURRENT_TIMESTAMP		ON UPDATE CURRENT_TIMESTAMP

id	user	token	access	details	last_c
1	test user 1	mZ84LPpcBl6PUqVRAlA1BBSTtzGgvdCzvP63io0BE9OYmqsD:	topic LIKE 'timestamp%'	This is test user 1 who has access to only timestamp topic data and any other subtopics under that	2018-

Figure 10-11. *Authentication table data schema*

As you can see, the *user* column is only for usernames, *token* holds actual API keys, and *access* holds our access control SQL condition. The field named *details* is for capturing information about the user and *last-change* holds the timestamp, which is automatically updated each time we update the record. The following is an explanation of the fields in a typical record entry in the table schema.

- **user**. Test user 1. This can be any alphanumeric username because it is the only placeholder for our purpose.

- **token**. A 64-byte random string generated from our own API, **/randomcode/**64. Instead of random code, we could also use the /uuid API; or it can be either of these, depending on the requirements. This can be used as a bearer token in an HTTP header while making any API requests.

- **access**. Here we are adding an actual query clause (so be careful what goes here) as **topic LIKE 'timestamp%**. This query clause ensures that when an authFilter is applied, the query is applicable only to topics that start with the word *timestamp*. This is how we control access to test-user-1 to only limited topics. The default value for this field is set to **0**, which will return **false** if included in the SQL query, and thus result in no records at the output.

- **details**. This is test user 1, who has access to only timestamp topic data and any subtopics under that.

This is a somewhat unconventional way to use the API key, but it is perfectly legal from a programming and coding perspective.

Adding Authentication Middleware

To implement this logic, we are going to modify the Node-RED settings. js file; and while we do that, we will need another Node.js module called mysql. Let's first install the module via command line, as follows.

```
# npm i mysql -g
```

Output

```
+ mysql@2.16.0
updated 1 package in 0.553s
```

Now open the settings.js file and search for the
httpNodeMiddleware section. As the comments for this section state, this
property can be used to add a custom middleware function in front of all
HTTP in nodes. This allows custom authentication to be applied to all
HTTP in nodes, or any other sort of common request processing.

Remove comments from this code block and update it with the
following code.

```
httpNodeMiddleware: function(req, res, next) {
    function getData(query, cbFunction){
        var connection = require('mysql').createConnection({
            host: 'localhost',
            user: '<your-database-username>',
            password: '<your-database-password>',
            database: 'tSeriesDB'
        });

        connection.query(query, function(err, rows, fields){
            if(err)
                cbFunction(false, err);
            else
                cbFunction(true, rows);
        });

        connection.end();
    }

    // get auth details from request header
    if(req.headers.authorization)
    {
```

```
    auth = Buffer.from(req.headers.authorization, 'ascii').
    toString();

    // split the string at space-character
    // typical auth header is like Bearer <access-token>
    req.authType = auth.split(' ')[0];
    req.userToken = auth.split(' ')[1];
}
else
{
    // take some actions if user is not authorized or
    provide only basic access
    req.authType = 'None';
    req.userToken = 'null';
}

getData('SELECT * FROM authTable WHERE token = \" + req.
userToken.toString() + '\' ORDER BY ID DESC LIMIT 1;',
function(code, data){
    // if data query is successful
    if(code === true)
    {
        // if authorization details are not available i.e.
        data.length === 0
        if(data.length === 0)
        {
            // set authFilter='0' if user authorization
            info is not available
            req.auth = false;
            req.authFilter= 0;
        }
        else
        {
```

```
                // use pass access string
                req.auth = true;
                req.authFilter = data[0].access;
            }

            // pass control to http node
            next();
        }
        else
        {
            // if there was an error, respond with 403 and
            terminate
            res.status(403).send("403: FORBIDDEN").end();
        }
    });
},
```

In the preceding code snippet, the middleware function does three main tasks.

First, it defines a user-defined function, which uses the MySQL library to connect with our time-series database and execute the supplied query. When query output is available or failed, the callback function is called with data and the status is passed to that function.

Second, middleware checks for an authorization header in every HTTP API request. If the access token is available, then it is captured in another variable and availability is set to true or false.

Once the token is captured, middleware checks for an access string in authTable, which is defined for the given token. This token, if available, is assigned to the authFilter variable, which we are using later for SQL query building. If no token was supplied, the filter will be set to '0', which will yield zero records upon query.

Enable and Test Authentication

Update settings.js appropriately, save it, and then restart Node-RED. Since Node-RED might have been already running with the forever utility, it is easy to restart it. Simply check for the PID of this process with the forever list command, and then send another command: forever restart **<PID>**. This restarts your Node-RED instance, and it reloads the updated settings.js file with authentication middleware code.

To test, let's first issue a simple cURL command without any authorization headers. With this command, we should get nothing in the output because authFilter is set to 0.

```
# curl -X GET https://www.in24hrs.xyz:1880/get/timestamp
```

Output 1
```
[]
```

```
# curl -X GET "https://www.in24hrs.xyz:1880/get/timestamp" -H
"Authorization: Bearer <token>"
```

Output 2
```
[{"id":149,"topic":"timestamp","payload":"partial-match",
"timestamp":"1544691441.578"}]
```

It is functioning as expected, and we are getting data only when we send the Bearer token. Now try adding a few more users with different *tokens* and change their *topic* access with simple SQL syntax. If you wish to provide access to multiple topics, use the OR operator to build the authFilter condition.

Our Core Platform Is Ready Now

While the message router has been represented as a separate block from a logical perspective, it is indeed an integrated functionality. And, we have done it in multiple passes throughout the last few chapters. The MQTT message broker, database listener, rule engine, and REST API all cater to form a functional message router.

Figure 10-12 shows the final set of blocks that we built; they are functional now.

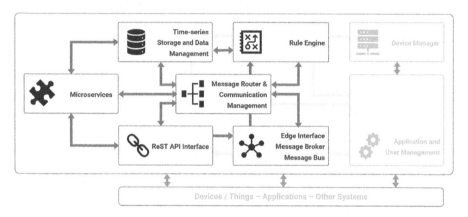

Figure 10-12. *Our own IoT platform core is now fully ready and functional*

The device manager and application/user management are essentially applications that can use our existing APIs for functioning. These applications can be developed and presented with a nice user interface for regular usage and device configurations to be attached to our IoT platform.

186

Summary

In this chapter, we created one of the critical blocks of our IoT platform. We also implemented authentication to our REST APIs, and thus secured them. Essentially, our core IoT platform is now ready.

In the next chapter, we see how to document our platform API and make it test-ready for developers. Going forward, this will also help you with regular testing of incremental changes in the platform, so that whenever you make a change to the API or message broker, or if you add a new API, testing can be done almost immediately in a convenient manner.

CHAPTER 11

Documentation and Testing

Good documentation accelerates the development and consumption of the developed resources. It also reduces the money and time that would otherwise be spent in answering support calls. The documentation is usually considered part of the overall user experience. Complete and accurate documentation is always a key to saving resources and improving the efficiency and effectiveness of API usage.

The obvious question stemming from this point is how can we document our IoT platform's API in an effective way? One of the most preferred ways is to use freely available or open source tools for documenting APIs. There are several options, which you can find at `https://nordicapis.com/ultimate-guide-to-30-api-documentation-solutions/`.

We will use Swagger tools for generating our API documentation. It is easy to create interactive documentation while effortlessly maintaining it on the go with Swagger. More importantly, you can either host the interface (definition and sandbox) on the Swagger hub, or you can integrate it as a standalone on an independent cloud instance. This is what we will do in our case.

In this chapter, we will

- Discuss how to prepare an OpenAPI specification

- Clone and update a Swagger package

- Test API docs in a live environment

© Anand Tamboli 2019
A. Tamboli, *Build Your Own IoT Platform*, https://doi.org/10.1007/978-1-4842-4498-2_11

Preparing a Valid OpenAPI Specification Document

The first step in creating useful documentation is to create an API description document in a valid format. Since Swagger uses OpenAPI specifications that can be documented using the YAML format, we will create that at the outset.

YAML (YAML Ain't Markup Language) is a human-readable data serialization language. It is commonly used for configuration files but could be used in many applications where data is being stored (e.g., debugging output) or transmitted (e.g., document headers).

If you are interested in learning more about the OpenAPI format and specifications, there are plenty of tutorials on the Internet. Some are easily available on the Swagger website as well.

The Swagger online editor is another open source and free tool that can be used to validate the specification document we are preparing; alternatively, we can make one from scratch in the same editor. This editor is available at `https://editor.swagger.io/#/`.

While writing this book, I created an API specification document (`api.yml`), which you can access from GitHub. Download the file, which is in `.yml` (i.e., YAML format). Paste the contents of the file into the Swagger online editor, and make sure that there are no warnings or errors. What you see in the view on the right of the Swagger editor is a fully functional user interface that will be the actual output after deployment.

You can play with the document, make some changes, and see how they affect the output. Once finished, you can copy and paste the file content back to the local copy for further usage.

Platform API Specification File Explained

Now let's refer to our platform API file contents and learn about the file structure in detail.

```
swagger: '2.0'
info:
  title: in24hrs.the.book
  description: This page provides documentation and also serves
  as a test sandbox for      **in24hrs** platform.
    **w:** [www.in24hrs.xyz](https://www.in24hrs.xyz)
    **e:** in24hrs@anandtamboli.com
  version: "1.0.1"
schemes:
  - https
host: 'www.in24hrs.xyz:1880'
basePath: /
```

The first line states the version of the API specification, which in our case is 2.0. The following lines provide some description about the document, which will also be shown on the user interface. We specified which API calling scheme our API will follow; it has been fixed to HTTPS only. The definitions of Host and basepath specify the base URL for our API.

Also note that any comments in this file begin with the # character, so the entire line is treated as a comment.

```
securityDefinitions:
  Bearer:
    type: apiKey
    name: authorization
    in: header
```

The next set of lines defines the security/authentication scheme for our API. In the previous chapter, we added a bearer authentication to our API and created a scheme where this has to be passed in the authorization header. These lines define this scheme such that when we use this interactive API UI, we can provide authentication details to it.

```
paths:
#----------------------------------------------------------------
# 1 Data publishing API
#----------------------------------------------------------------
  /pub/{topic}/{payload}:
    post:
      description: 'create a new data {payload} for a {topic}'
      security:
        - Bearer: []
      tags:
        - '1 Data publishing API'
      parameters:
        - name: topic
          in: path
          description: 'Topic to publish data for'
          type: string
          required: true
        - name: payload
          in: path
          description: 'Message payload for given topic, could
          be plain text, binary, json, or any other format'
          type: string
          required: true
      responses:
        '200':
          description: 'Response to post/publish operation'
```

```
schema:
  type: object
  properties:
    success:
      type: boolean
      description: 'Success status of operation'
    message:
      type: object
      description: 'Additional response text'
```

After those base definitions, we start defining our API's endpoints. Our first data publishing API /pub is shown here. Notice how we have enabled authentication for the first API, and subsequently, this will be used for each API definition.

The rest of the contents are self-explanatory, which is also an advantage due to the usage of the YAML format. You can use any text editor for editing this file locally; however, I recommend online editing using the Swagger UI editor because it can help you check for errors and warnings while you edit. As a next step, head over to the Swagger UI GitHub page at https://github.com/swagger-api/swagger-ui. Then, click Clone or the Download button, and select the Download ZIP option, refer to Figure 11-1 for more details. Download the files to a convenient location on your computer and extract them.

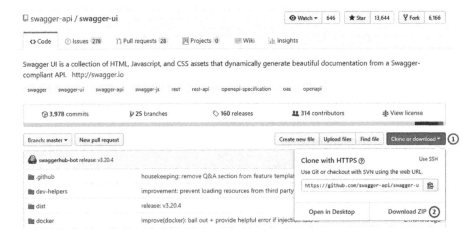

Figure 11-1. *Download Swagger-UI files to your local computer*

Since we are not going to compile the source, but only use the UI part of it, we will not need the entire downloaded package. Locate the dist folder in extracted files. Copy and paste this folder out of the main folder and place it in a standalone directory. At this point, you can safely delete the rest of the extracted package if you wish to.

Preparing Distribution Package for Final Upload

At this stage, if you already downloaded the api.yml file, place this file in the dist folder that we separated. There is a file named index.html in the dist folder, which now can be opened for editing in any text editor.

Locate the JavaScript section in the index.html file and edit it as follows.

```
const ui = SwaggerUIBundle({
url: "http://petstore.swagger.io/v2/swagger.json",
dom_id: '#swagger-ui',
```

Change the URL to our API specification file as

```
const ui = SwaggerUIBundle({
url: "api.yml",
dom_id: '#swagger-ui',
```

Now let's change the name of the folder (from `dist`) to `docs` for convenience; you can change it to any name you want though. With this change, our API specification package is ready for upload.

Upload API Docs and Make It Live

Now connect to our cloud instance over FTTP using FileZilla or any other FTTP tool and upload this (`docs`) folder to the `/var/www/html/` directory. This is our cloud instance's web directory and our `index.php` file should be visible here already. Once all the files are uploaded, head over to the cloud instance web URL (`www.in24hrs.xyz/docs`) in your browser and see for yourself. Our API documentation is now live and should look similar to what is shown in Figure 11-2.

Note the Authorize button at the top of the API. It is for providing authorization details to the UI. If you use the API now, especially the data reading API, you will not get anything in the output, because not providing authentication yields empty output.

The lock icons on each of the API listings indicate that authorization is required.

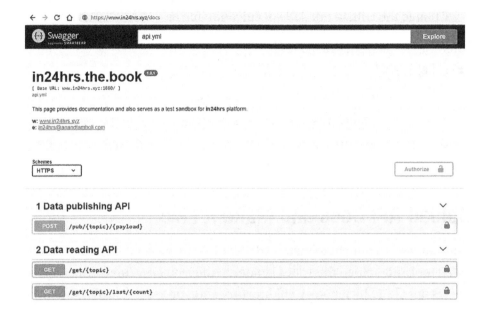

Figure 11-2. *Live API documentation page*

Authorize and Test API

In Chapter 10, we established a token-based API authorization and authentication. This expects an authorization header with contents as Bearer <token>, where token is an alphanumeric string used for a unique identification of the API caller.

To provide this information in our live Swagger UI, click the Authorize button, which opens an authorizations dialog box asking for value input, as shown in Figure 11-3. Note that we are adding the keyword, Bearer, at the beginning of this value input with a space, followed by our access token. Once we press the Authorize button, the dialog box will show that you are logged in with given authorization information. The lock icons on the API headings change, as shown in Figure 11-3.

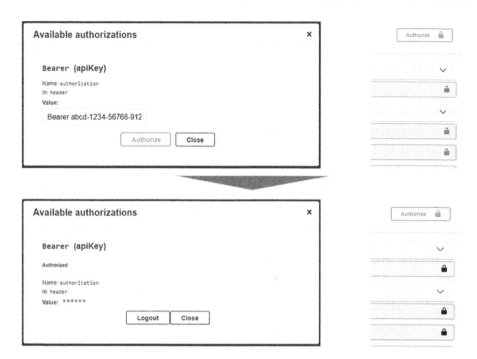

Figure 11-3. *Providing authorization in Swagger UI*

If you want to test with a different authorization token, simply click the Authorize button, press Logout, and reauthorize with the new token.

There are several UI configuration parameters, which are explained in the Swagger documentation. These parameters could be utilized to make this UI more interactive and customized to your liking. It will not affect or change anything in the API specification file. If you spend enough time beautifying it, you can take it to a whole new level. However, at this stage, you should be able to test various APIs in our IoT platform on this page.

We now have our API clearly documented and available for developers or users to test interactively. Whenever you add any new endpoint to the platform, you can update the YAML definition in the api.yml file, and the UI will update with a new set of specifications.

Summary

In this chapter, we discussed the documentation method and created an API document for our own platform. Until this point, we had a fully working IoT platform along with the required documentation and all the core functionalities that we planned in the initial chapters. We also established a good and extensible framework, which we can keep improving and expanding as the development, usage, and overall business progresses without disrupting what is working.

In the next chapter, we review what we did throughout, and more importantly, why we did it! I also address a few commonly asked questions in various forums and discuss a few advancements that are in progress, which you might want to add to the platform when you build it.

## CHAPTER 12

What We Built and the Takeaways

What we did in last the 11 chapters has always been painted as a hazy picture by many—only to prevent people from taking charge and building their own platform as they deemed fit. As any sane person would do, we started by learning the landscape of the Internet of Things and then slowly delved into the specifics of it.

By Chapter 3, we had a fair idea of what is required to build our own IoT platform, and we created a detailed version of the requirements in the subsequent chapter. It becomes much simpler to execute a plan once the goals and directions are clear. So, we were able to swiftly move through that phase of building our own platform's core.

Understanding a few topologies and technologies, such as MQTT, has been a key to development, which we did in Chapter 6. Knowing more about MQTT not only helped with building the message broker for the platform, but it has also opened many other opportunities for live, two-way communication across several systems, applications, and devices. This can open doors to many new applications and solutions.

In subsequent steps, we built various APIs and microservices, and we addressed the security aspects as we progressed. Ending with the interactive documentation, we accomplished the task of building our own IoT platform.

© Anand Tamboli 2019
A. Tamboli, *Build Your Own IoT Platform*, https://doi.org/10.1007/978-1-4842-4498-2_12

The process by itself would have taken less than 24 hours to build the platform and get it up and running. This is contrary to what many would tell you when you ask, "How long will it take to build my own IoT platform?" Although we are not boasting a full-blown, massive IoT platform, the developed version is just a few steps away from being one, and this is a significant stepping stone.

Increasing Security for the Cloud Instance

While we have established a firewall, SSL, and many other things, securing the cloud instance is a separate exercise. The principles that you should apply in securing a cloud instance are the same as those you would apply in securing any other operating system, whether it is virtual (cloud) or real (in-premise).

The following are a few pointers and strategies that you can explore to increase security for the cloud instance.

- Enabling and reviewing audit logs is one of the best practices that you can follow, and it does not require anything to set up explicitly. The stacks we have installed are already taking care of it.

- For the entire process, we utilized the root access of the system. This does not have to be that way, however; you can disable the root access permanently if you want to.

- One of the many annoying things you notice while maintaining your own cloud instance is *bots*! There are several programs that constantly scavenge for open ports or access and install malware or exploit another free machine. Our firewall restricts these bots from accessing important resources; however, a few essential ports cannot be closed. Ports such as SSH, MQTT, and other web-facing APIs need to be open.

A clever strategy that people deploy in securing an SSH port is to change the default port from 22 to something conspicuous. Although many experts would advise that this is not the best strategy, believe me, it works because it adds one more hurdle to nuisance creators. Combine it with SSH keys, and you are good to go.

Some people would go a step further and introduce the *port knocking* mechanism, which makes it extremely difficult (and near impossible) to break in via SSH access.

- Adding programs like fail2ban or mod-security is also a helpful strategy for improving security. These programs monitor log files and detect potential attacks. Based on the rules you set up, these programs can blacklist attacking IPs or ban or rate limit them for a short period of time.

- In addition to securing a cloud instance, you may also consider encryption of data (in flight or at rest) as a potential strategy. This has clear overheads involved, such as encryption/decryption while storing and retrieving data, which may also increase the packet size in transit. However, a pragmatic decision has to be made, and then this strategy can be put in place on the top of the core platform infrastructure.

In general, no security strategy is enough for an ever-changing and evolving cyber world; however, you must start somewhere, and that depends on what you want to achieve from your infrastructure. It absolutely depends on each situation.

What About SQL Injection Through APIs?

Remember that *security* is a very vague term. Just because we have a secured API with SSL and authentication does not mean it is secure. Adding some type of encryption on both ends (sending and receiving) hardens it further. However, this is something beyond the scope of this book, as we are only establishing a core platform for that exchange. What is exchanged is still open. The platform exchanges encrypted messages just the same as non-encrypted messages without any fuss.

However, one of the nagging questions you might have had throughout the exercise of building the platform involves SQL injection. Again, you can only go so far. One basic fix that needs to be applied in our code is to escape any inputs we are getting from API calls. This is an easy fix. The following snippet shows how to apply it. This snippet is taken from the database listener's `create` query functional node.

```
// database-listener create-query code
...
var mysql = context.global.mysql;

var strQuery = "INSERT INTO thingData (topic, payload, timestamp,
              deleted) VALUES (" + mysql.escape(msg.topic) +
              "," + mysql.escape(msg.payload) + ",'" +
              timestamp + "', 0);";
...
```

In the preceding snippet, code that is marked in **bold** are new additions. We have already installed a MySQL package. The code block calls it from `global` context of Node-RED and captures it in another variable called `mysql`. We are then simply using the `mysql.escape` function to escape user input, which is one of the many standard practices for avoiding SQL injection.

To get this package accessible in Node-RED's global context, we must modify the settings.js file slightly. Open the settings.js file and locate code block for functionGlobalContext. Modify this code block to look like the following:

```
// Anything in this hash is globally available to all
    functions.
// It is accessed as context.global.
// eg:
//    functionGlobalContext: { os:require('os') }
// can be accessed in a function block as:
//    context.global.os
functionGlobalContext: {
   // accessible as context.global.mysql
   mysql: require('mysql')
},
```

Save the file and restart Node-RED to put this change into effect. Now, when you deploy the flow with changes in the create-query functional node, SQL-escaping will be effective. The same change can be applied to all the query blocks on our API flow sequence.

Should We Have Used MongoDB Instead of MySQL?

Quite frankly, we had to start somewhere, and MySQL was a stable choice. MongoDB can be used in place of MySQL too, which will call for changes in the data schema and some of the code structure.

However, as far as the architecture of the core platform is concerned, it will not change at all. There are several tutorials and blogs that compare MongoDB and MySQL. These articles explain features and function-level differences and discuss where to use these databases. Interestingly, the IoT platform is an application that sits at the crossroads of many of those suggestions. You could go either way and still be right.

In a nutshell, start with MySQL and then include MongoDB as you grow. This will not break things later, and it will be a one-time exercise to change over.

I strongly believe that a lack of features is not a lack of functionality. What we have built is absolutely essential and mandatory, without which it will not be an IoT platform. Anything else, that we wish to add can be regarded as a feature that can be added on the top whenever required.

Some Experts Might Still Try to Talk You Out of This

Let them! That is all I can say at the outset; however, think deeply about why others are trying to talk you out of building your own IoT platform. What is their argument? If you clearly understand the argument behind the suggestion to buy an off-the-shelf platform rather than build your own, then it will make better sense. Off-the-shelf platforms are popular and have cool features, and big companies are behind them—but these are weak arguments.

One of the key problems with freemium and off-the-shelf platforms is a *lock-in*. Even if it claims to be easy to detach and go elsewhere, in practice, it is far from easy to do this. You would be better off building your own than carrying the risk of being locked in. There is also the threat of having a legacy lock-in; that is, you will find it extremely difficult and expensive to change the underlying technology in the middle. Once you are set, that is it: no changes until you upgrade. This is not a good choice in my opinion.

But, if you are not interested in the ongoing maintenance of your own platform, no matter how small that may be, you may want to think twice.

If your business needs a high level of control and high levels of security over the data and overall infrastructure, building your own is the best option. Let the experts know this.

The amount of money that you want to spend on building your own platform vs. the amount that you can save by buying off the shelf or by subscribing is a classic argument. Many experts do not account the total cost of ownership (TCO). This builds up over time, and at the outset, justifies the contrary decision. And the argument that managing your own platform consumes valuable time, while a managed platform gives you time to do other business is a fallacy. You end up managing managed platforms in one way or another without realizing it. So, the proposition is not so different after all. If you are having second thoughts, do the cost-benefit analysis over a longer term, like seven to ten years, and then see what makes sense. If the subscription or buying option is still lucrative, make the move.

See who these experts are and check where their vested interests lie. Seek independent opinions, do the objective evaluations, and then make the call.

How Is Our Platform Different from AWS, Google, and Azure?

Just on the basis of true merit, our platform is as good as AWS, Google, or Azure; functionally, they all compare about the same. However, it is not entirely an apples-to-apples comparison. The following are a few reasons why.

- AWS, Google, and Azure are fundamentally cloud services—IoT as well as others, whereas what we have is a purpose-built IoT platform core.

- Cloud computing is a majority part of the others' offerings; whereas in our case, the IoT core is the central function and cloud computing is the support function.

- The other platforms are essentially built as jack-of-all types. We have a vertical-specific IoT platform that is intended to be service or product specific upon extension.

- The other platforms mainly boast various features and add-ons, which are "good to have" things on the IoT platform but may not be required for all IoT products or services. On the other hand, we have exactly what each IoT product and service needs at the minimum.

- All of the others are managed platforms, whereas we are managing our own (or you can outsource it). From a price standpoint, they are all about the same when compared in parity.

- Offerings like instant provisioning, autoscaling, compliance, security, and overall management are at par whether you build your own or buy.

- Our build has the benefit of being purposefully built, it can be low power, and it is very customizable. It is not inherently multisite nor does it have redundancy, as the cloud services do.

There may not be like-to-like comparisons with the scale or size of the platform; however, if you are looking at it from the perspective of your own requirements, the comparison is simpler.

There Is a New Version of MQTT

The MQTT version used to build our IoT platform is 3.1.1, which was the latest version at the time of my writing this book. MQTT version 5.0 was released in October 2018. Although the specifications were released, brokers and client implementations were not yet available.

While version 3.1.1 is still the most stateful and scalable IoT protocol, with millions of simultaneous connections as a benchmark, the newer version is designed to make it easier to scale to immense amounts of concurrent connections.

The following are some of the enhancements in MQTT v5.0.

- Enhancements in scalability for large-scale systems

- Improved error reporting with negative acknowledgments and error codes

- A capability discovery mechanism to let clients know what a broker is (and is not) capable of

- Request-response behavior with the publish/subscribe mechanism

- Shared subscriptions among multiple clients (cluster of clients)

- *Time to live* (TTL) for messages and client sessions (such that a retained message could expire after a specified time)

The Eclipse Paho project is driving most of the development to bring MQTT v5.0 clients and brokers, along with many other (open source and other) players. While MQTT v5.0 does not have a significant advantage over v3.1.1, it does solve some problems in specific situations. So, if you think this might be the case for you, keep an eye on the latest developments. Even if it is not of direct interest to you, seeing v5.0 in action could spark some possibilities.

My Platform Is Ready. Now What?

The first thing you should do with your own IoT platform is develop a sample application. Why? Because it will give you a better idea from a full cycle standpoint and may highlight issues in the build. It may show what is not adding up or what is missing. Accordingly, you may have to fine-tune a few things to suit your requirements.

More importantly, when you develop a sample application, it serves as a boilerplate for the next few applications. The sample application also works like a sandbox for testing new things and changes while we make it. So, even if you have a final application that is waiting to be developed, spend a little more time to work on a sample app; it will help in the long run.

Additionally, you can extend APIs and microservices to your liking; add more authentication methods and checks for your platform access, or build a user and device management app to ease out future requirements.

The Next Big Thing

Emerging technologies are still emerging, and the Internet of Things is still finding its ground, marching toward the maturity it deserves. If you wish to make this platform bigger and even more powerful, try standing up multiple instances and create a high-availability infrastructure.

Use MQTT bridges and connect with other platforms for interoperability. You can also run multiple MQTT instances on the same cloud with different ports and effectively separate various applications per port while using the same platform core. This can help you create a multitenant infrastructure for your multiple applications and keep them away from data contamination.

Learn and integrate tensor flow into the platform to add machine learning capabilities. This can take your platform to a different usability and utility level.

The possibilities are endless when you have such a powerful core infrastructure ready, and it is in your full control.

If You Need to Find More Resources

The Internet is a one-stop shop in this case. Node-RED forums and NPM websites are places you should frequent. This is mainly because our platform heavily leverages these two technologies.

Additionally, since the core architecture is now in place, adding more technologies and protocols is not going to be a problem. Whether it is including MongoDB to the platform (and there is Node-RED node for that) or implementing encryption/decryption of data in-flight or at rest, depending on the technology you want to utilize, the search-ground may change, but eventually, they wire up nicely together to make the platform more powerful; one that is your own!

Finally...

One of my many objectives for writing this book was to provide a step-by-step guide on building something that is quite valuable and yet not openly available. I have interacted with several clients and colleagues who are dismayed because searching "how to build your own IoT platform" does not yield anything useful. I hope this book has helped you find something useful in this context.

To me, this is not the end, but the beginning of your self-sufficiency in emerging technologies, and for this, I wish you all the best!

Glossary

Advanced Message Queuing Protocol (AMQP): An open application layer protocol for message-oriented middleware with a focus on queuing, routing (P2P, pub/sub), security, and reliability.

Bluetooth Low Energy (BLE): A wireless personal area network (PAN) aimed at devices with reduced power consumption and cost while maintaining a similar communication range to regular Bluetooth.

Constrained Application Protocol (CoAP): An application layer protocol used in resource-constrained devices that allows Internet connectivity and remote control.

Edge gateway: The connecting factor between device analytics and cloud data processing and analytics.

Edge layer: An architectural shift in IoT that breaks the norm of the traditional client-server model. This is the first layer of connectivity for devices to connect to before going to the server. Responsible for the local connectivity of devices and for managing the data collection and connection to this server.

Embedded device/systems: A computer with a dedicated function within a larger mechanical or electrical system that is embedded as part of a complete device.

Flow-based programming: A type of programming that defines applications as networks of the process that exchanges data across defined connections by message passing, where the connections are specified externally to the processes.

© Anand Tamboli 2019
A. Tamboli, *Build Your Own IoT Platform*, https://doi.org/10.1007/978-1-4842-4498-2

Internet of Things (IoT): A network of objects (such as sensors and actuators) that can capture data autonomously and self-configure intelligently based on physical world events, allowing these systems to become active participants in various public, commercial, scientific, and personal processes.

IoT cloud platform: A cloud platform that provides a set of services that simplify the integration process between the services provided by cloud platforms and IoT devices. Some platforms include development tools and data analytics capabilities.

Lightweight protocol: Any protocol that has a lesser and leaner payload when being used and transmitted over a network connection.

LoRaWAN (Long Range Wide Area Network): LoRa is a patented digital wireless data communication technology. It uses license-free sub-gigahertz radio frequency bands like 169 MHz, 433 MHz, 868 MHz (Europe and India), and 915 MHz (North America). LoRa enables very long-range transmissions and is presented in two parts: LoRa, the physical layer, and LoRaWAN, the upper layers. LoRaWAN is the network on which LoRa operates and can be used by IoT for remote and unconnected industries. LoRaWAN is a media access control (MAC) layer protocol but mainly is a network layer protocol for managing communication between LPWAN gateways and end-node devices as a routing protocol maintained by the LoRa Alliance.

Machine-to-machine (M2M): Refers to a network setup that allows connected devices to communicate freely, usually between a large number of devices. M2M often refers to the use of distributed systems in industrial and manufacturing applications.

Message Queuing Telemetry Transport (MQTT): A lightweight messaging protocol that runs on the TCP/IP protocol. It is designed for communicating with small devices in remote locations with low network bandwidth.

Narrowband IoT (NB-IoT): A low-power wide-area network (LPWAN) radio technology standard developed by 3GPP to enable a wide range of cellular devices and services. NB-IoT focuses specifically on indoor coverage, low cost, long battery life, and high connection density. NB-IoT uses a subset of the LTE standard but limits the bandwidth to a single narrow band of 200 kHz.

Transmission Control Protocol/Internet Protocol (TCP/IP): A basic client-server model communication protocol for the Internet and private networks.

YAML (YAML Ain't Markup Language): A human-readable data serialization language. It is commonly used for configuration files but could be used in many applications where data is being stored (e.g., debugging output) or transmitted (e.g., document headers).

Note   All definitions and terms are adopted from various sources on the Internet, including Wikipedia.

References

- https://dzone.com/articles/iot-glossary-terms-you-need-to-know

- https://en.m.wikipedia.org/wiki/

- https://iotos.io/en/news/iot-glossary/

- www.aeris.com/iot-dictionary/?name_directory_startswith=I

Index

Made in the USA
Monee, IL
06 May 2020